Bookkeeping and Accounting Terms

Anthony Nielsen

Chambers Commercial Reference

© W & R Chambers Ltd Edinburgh, 1987

Published by W & R Chambers Ltd Edinburgh, 1987

We have made every effort to mark as such all words which we believe to be trademarks. We should also like to make it clear that the presence of a word in this book, whether marked or unmarked, in no way affects its legal status as a trademark.

British Library Cataloguing in Publication Data
Nielsen, Anthony
    Bookkeeping and accounting terms.—
    (Chambers commercial reference series)
    1. Accounting—Dictionaries
    I. Title
    657'.03'21   HF5621
ISBN 0-550-18062-1

Typeset by Outline
Printed in Singapore by Singapore National Printers Ltd.

Preface

Bookkeeping and Accounting Terms is a compact but comprehensive reference book which has been specially written to meet the needs of school and college students on a wide range of business and vocational courses at intermediate level.

Along with the other titles in the Chambers Commercial Reference series, *Bookkeeping and Accounting Terms* provides up-to-date explanations of the key terms used in various areas of business activity. All words and abbreviations are listed alphabetically and defined in clear simple English.

Although intended as a companion to course studies, *Bookkeeping and Accounting Terms* is also an ideal reference text for those already working in a commercial environment. The book will prove to be an invaluable companion to their work.

Bookkeeping and Accounting Terms

Anthony Nielsen has been a practising Chartered Accountant and principal partner in a firm for many years. In addition to his professional activities with the firm he has lectured on accounting, taxation, auditing and computing. He has continually emphasised the need for practical experience within the accounting field.

Aa

ACA (1) Associate of the Institute of Chartered Accountants in England and Wales. (2) Associate of the Institute of Chartered Accountants in Ireland. See also **chartered accountant**.

ACCA Associate of the Chartered Association of Certified Accountants. See also **certified accountant**.

account A section of the ledger in which a record is made of every transaction relating to the same activity. Individual accounts are opened for every debtor and creditor, and for each heading of expense, income, asset and liability.

account classes The major classes (or groups) into which accounts are divided. There are *personal, nominal* and *real* accounts.

account codes The numbers allocated to individual accounts to give unique recognition when they are used with computerised or mechanised accounting systems. See also **folio references.**

account sales A document concerned with consignment accounts. It is sent by an agent to the principal, showing the income from the goods sold on the principal's behalf, less expenses and commission of the agent.

accountant A person whose work involves the collection, recording, analysis and interpretation of the financial details of a company's operations. A qualified accountant is a member of a **recognised accountancy body**. See also **certified accountant, chartered accountant, cost and management accountant** and **public finance accountant**.

accounting concept Same as **concept of accounting**.

accounting conventions   Same as **conventions**.

accounting machine   A mechanically or electrically operated device which will process accounting information and print required details.

accounting period   (1) The amount of time specified as the basis for measuring the results of business in terms of profit or loss. This is a period of twelve months except (usually) for the first or last period of trading. (2) The twelve month accounting period is usually divided into thirteen 4-week periods or twelve calendar month periods for purposes of financial control.

account payee   See **crossed cheques**.

accounting ratio   A method of measuring the size relationship of one item to another item.

accounting reference date   The date which marks the end of a limited company's accounting period.

accounting reference period   The accounting period of a limited company.

accounts payable   The accounts of creditors (to whom money is owed).

accounts receivable   The accounts of debtors (from whom money is due).

accrual   An expense unpaid at the accounting period end for which a specific invoice is not issued. It is not entered in the creditor's account but shown as a liability on the relevant expense account. An accrual is shown under the heading 'Current liabilities' in the balance sheet as *expenses owing* or *accrued expenses*, e.g. rent due. Same as **expenses outstanding, expenses owing, accrued charges** and **accrued expenses**.

accruals concept   Same as **matching concept**.

accrued charges   Same as **accrual**.

accrued expenses   Same as **accrual**.

accrued income   Income, other than from sales, which is due but has not been received at the end of the accounting period. It is not shown in the debtor's account but is shown as a debit balance on the relevant income account. Accrued incomes are shown under the heading 'Current assets' in the balance sheet as sundry debtors, e.g. rent receivable, fees or interest receivable. Same as **accrued receipts**.

accrued receipt   Same as **accrued income**.

accumulated fund   The investment made by members of a non-profit-making organisation in that organisation. The fund represents the amount that would be paid back to existing members if the club or society was to close down. It is sometimes referred to as **capital** or **capital fund**.

acid test ratio   This is recognised as the critical liquidity ratio. It measures the cash and bank balances (plus other easily and quickly realisable investments) as a ratio of current liabilities. It is calculated as follows:
acid test ratio = cash+bank balances : current liabilities

ACMA   Associate of the Institute of Cost and Management Accountants. See also **cost and management accountant**.

adjusting entries   Same as **adjustments**.

adjustments   Entries made in the ledger after the trial balance has been prepared. These entries are additions and amendments caused by, for example, accruals, prepayments, alterations to provisions, corrections for errors and adjustments to the owner's drawings account.

advice note   A document sent by the supplier of goods to the buyer advising that goods ordered have been despatched to him.

ageing schedule (of debtors)   A list of debtors and the amounts they owe, analysed according to the length of time that the debts have been owing. Using such a schedule, provision can be made for bad debts or action can be taken to collect overdue sums.

3

Analysed Book Layout (Credit Side Only)
Cash Book of B. Maddison

Date 19-9	Details	FOLIO	1 Bank	2 Cash	3 Materials	4 Petrol, Oil	5 Drawings	6 Misc	7 VAT	2b
May 1	B&Q	^	594·41		516·90				77·51	
" 3	Postage	GL P4		8·26				8·26		
" 8	B.Telecom	GL T1	147·92					128·63	19·29	
" 15	Cash	^	200·00				200·00			
" 16	Petrol	^		20·00		17·39			2·61	
" 19	Robert Ltd	PL R3	132·00					132·00		
" 19	Glass Co.	^	162·33		141·16				21·17	
" 19	Putty Ltd	^		25·19	21·91				3·28	
" 22	Cash	^	200·00				200·00			
" 23	Petrol	^		20·00		17·39			2·61	
" 23	H.B. Blg Soc	^	251·62				251·62			
" 23	Insurance	GL I2	204·80					204·80		
" 26	D.I.Y. Co.	^	673·24		585·45				87·79	
" 30	Petrol	^		20·00		17·39			2·61	
" 31	Inland Rev	^	982·31				982·31			
" 31	Bal.	c/d	1342·07	85·61				1427·68		
			4758·70	179·06	1265·42	52·17	1633·93	1769·37	216·87	
			^	^	GLM3	GLM2	GLD1	^	GLV1	

The Balance c/d figure is also entered in the Miscellaneous column to enable the totals of columns 3 to 7 to be cross cast and checked with the total of columns 1 and 2.

Folio references refer to the account in the ledger to which an entry has been posted —

> GL is General ledger
> D1 is Drawings account
> I2 is Insurance
> M2 is Motor expenses account
> M3 is Materials
> P4 is Postage, packing & stationery
> T1 is Telephone account
> V1 is VAT account

^means that no posting is required for that individual entry or total.

Further analysis columns could be used for Payments to creditors, Wages, Sub contract payments or any regularly occurring payments. See General Ledger Account Layout (page 47) for posting of May petrol total.

agent   A person (or company) who has the authority and power to act on behalf of his or her principal.

allocated stock   The quantity of stock that needs to be set aside to meet the known requirements of the organisation or specific customer orders.

allotment of shares   The process of allocating shares available for issue to those who have applied for them, and the notification to applicants of their allocation.

allowances   (1) Reductions in the invoiced price of goods allowed by the seller, e.g. to allow for damaged goods, delay in delivery, goods delivered slightly different to those ordered.   (2) Reductions in the account of a debtor to allow for containers returned or goods returned by him. Allowances are shown by the issue of a credit note, which is used as a source document for bookkeeping.

amalgamation   The joining together of two or more separate businesses to form one business.

amortisation   (1) The writing-off of an asset. (2) This term is usually used when referring to the depreciation of an asset which will depreciate by effluxion of time, e.g. a lease. Thus sums of money are set aside, equivalent to the depreciation, to provide for the asset's replacement. See also **sinking fund** and **sinking fund investment account**.

analysed book   A book which contains columns to enable a business to analyse the financial details recorded therein. Such a book may be a day book (analysing sales and purchases between different categories of goods), a petty cash book or a cash book. See illustration on page 4.

annual budget   The financial implications of planned activities for a year. See also **budget**.

annuity   (1) A lump sum purchase of a future guaranteed income.   (2) A series of equal payments from an investment.

application for shares   A limited company, whether public or private, has the power to obtain finance by

5

seeking investors. A public company must issue a prospectus and this usually contains an application form for shares. The prospectus, which may appear in newspapers in the form of an advertisement, is inviting prospective investors to apply for shares. A private company cannot advertise its share offer in the same way, but prospective investors (known and acceptable to the promoter, directors or existing shareholders) must nevertheless apply for shares.

applications software Computer programs which are designed to perform a specific job, e.g. a stock control program or word-processing program. See also **package**.

appreciation The increase in the value of assets due to: (a) increasing scarcity; (b) improvement with age; (c) antique value; (d) loss in the value of money.

appropriation The taking of and/or the dividing of assets as in 'the appropriation of a person's belongings'. In accounting terms it refers to the dividing of profits between (a) partners; (b) the shareholders and the state (in the case of a company). In both cases the division of profits is shown in an account called the appropriation account.

appropriation account An account in a partnership or company which is used to show allocation of profits.

articles of association Details which need to be filed with the Registrar of Companies upon the formation (sometimes called registration) of a company are described in the articles of association. They contain the internal regulations of the company and are akin to the 'Rule Book' of a club or society.

asset Any item of value belonging to a business. This includes money owed to the business.

asset account An account which records the transactions relating to an asset so that the value of the asset can be seen. This value is normally the cost price and represents the investment by the business in that asset. It may not indicate its saleable value.

asset ledger   The ledger which records the accounts of fixed assets.

asset turnover ratio   This is the ratio of sales (turnover) to total assets. The ratio is usually expressed as a number which is calculated as follows:

$$\text{asset turnover ratio} = \frac{\text{sales}}{\text{total assets}}$$

This ratio is a measure of how effectively the business is using its total assets to generate sales.

asset types   These are: **current asset; fictitious asset; fixed asset; intangible asset; tangible asset**.

audit   An audit is an examination of the financial records and the accounts prepared from them, to verify their accuracy or otherwise. An audit will also normally involve a physical check on stocks and other assets to prove that they actually exist. The Companies Act requires all limited companies to present audited accounts to their shareholders.

auditor   A person who carries out an audit. In the case of a limited company the auditor is appointed by the shareholders and must be a member of a recognised accountancy body.

auditor's report   Having completed an audit, the auditor must sign a statement to that effect. The statement, or report, must indicate the auditor's opinion as to the accuracy of the accounts audited and whether they show a 'true and fair' view, indicating any inaccuracies or areas about which the auditor is doubtful or concerned. In the case of a limited company, since the auditor is appointed by the shareholders, the report is presented to them and it is attached to the accounts prepared by the directors.

authorised capital   The capital with which a company is registered upon formation. This capital is the amount that the company is allowed to issue if it desires to do so. The authorised capital can be altered by shareholders passing the appropriate resolution, which is then filed with the Registrar of Companies.

average cost (AVCO)   See **pricing methods, weighted average.**

average stock   The quantity and value of stock that a business would normally expect to have. For working out stock turnover rates, the average value of stock held would need to be calculated. If a continuous inventory system operates, the average stock could be accurately obtained by averaging, for example, the month-end stock values during the year. Where no stock control procedures exist, an average of the opening stock value and the closing stock value is the only way of calculating the figure.

Bb

bad debt   An amount owing to a business which is considered unobtainable and is therefore treated as a loss.

balance   The difference between the debit and credit sides of an account.

balance sheet   A statement which shows the assets and liabilities of a business on a specific date. The balance sheet acts as a summary of the financial state of affairs and one is always included with the final accounts. Company law requires a balance sheet to be given to shareholders. See illustration on page 10.

balancing accounts   This means calculating the balance on an account. To do this, both the credit and debit sides are totalled and the difference between the two sides is the balance. This balance, (if written), is shown on the side with the lesser amount as the balance carried down (c/d), and is also shown beneath the ruled total on the side with the greater amount as the balance brought down (b/d).

bank account   (1) Money deposited with a bank for safekeeping is recorded by the bank in a bank account. The person or business putting the money in the bank (called the depositor or the account holder) can withdraw money either by cheque — if the money is in a current account — or by presenting the bank pass book if the money is in a deposit account.   (2) The business record of the money deposited in the bank. This usually refers to the current account only.

bank book   Same as **bank pass book.**

Balance Sheet Layout

B. MADDISON

T/A B. MADDISON (GLAZIERS)

Balance Sheet as at 31st July 1987

Fixed Assets

	£ Cost	£ Depn	£ WDV
Motor Van	2290	572	1718
Motor Car (1)	2675	1290	1385
Motor Car (2)	950	475	475
Tools & Equipment	350	349	1
Office Equipment	38	8	30
	6303	2694	3609
less H.P. outstanding			1000
			2609

Current Assets

Debtors		1300	
Deposit A/C		521	
VAT		805	
		2626	

Less Current Liabilities

Bank O/D	730		
Creditors	360		
Receipts in advance	1150	2240	387
			£2996

Financed By

B. Maddison Capital (1/8/86)		3135
Add: Profit	6071	
Less: Drawings	7647	(1576)
		1559
Add: Loans (1)	937	
(2)	500	1437
		£2996

10

bank cash book If a business uses a current account for all its payments, except small cash items which are recorded in a petty cash book, then the business bank account is kept in a bank cash book.

bank charges Banks charge their customers for provision of a current account service. Charges are also made for providing financial services, such as investment advice, agreeing loans and taxation advice. Same as **service charges** and **bank commission.**

bank giro credit Same as **credit transfer.**

bank interest (1) A payment made by a bank to a depositor for the use of the depositor's money. Money deposited with a bank is used by the bank to earn income by providing loans and overdrafts. Out of this income a depositor will receive the return called interest. (2) The amount charged by a bank to a borrower.

bank loan An amount lent by a bank to a borrower for a specific period at an agreed rate of interest.

bank overdraft Same as **overdraft.**

bank pass book A book which records details of money kept in a bank deposit account and which must be presented for any deposit or withdrawal of money. Same as **bank book.**

bank reconciliation statement A statement which shows why and how the bank account balance in the business cash book differs from the balance shown on the bank statement after all transactions to date have been entered in the cash book.

bank reference A businessman who is seeking to establish the creditworthiness of a prospective customer may ask the customer to provide a bank reference. Since a bank will only give a reference to another bank, the businessman's bank must approach the customer's bank.

bank statement A summary, provided by the bank, of the transactions on a customer's account. Statements are provided at the frequency requested by the customer — monthly, weekly, or daily.

banker's order   Same as **standing order**.

bankruptcy   A person is declared bankrupt by a court. All his remaining assets with a few exceptions are seized, sold and distributed evenly amongst the creditors.

bar account   An account which will show the profit and loss made by the 'bar' providing drinks and other refreshments. Often found in the accounts of non-profit-making organisations.

batch control   Where large volumes of source documents exist in use with a computer system, a method of control is necessary to ensure documents do not go astray. Batch control is one such method where documents are kept in separate groups or batches (e.g. of 20, 50 or 100); these are pre-listed and totalled, numbered, registered and monitored at all stages of their processing.

Bin Card

CARD NO.	**BIN CARD**	STOCK NO.		
DESCRIPTION *Plastic Moulded Handle*		LOCATION		
		UNIT OF ISSUE		
Date	Document Ref.	Received	Issued	Balance
May 4	*GRN 3456*	*50*		*50*
14	*MR 999*		*30*	*20*
June 5	*MR 1062*		*10*	*10*
12	*GRN 4567*	*40*		*50*

bill   (1) A written statement of — in the case of an invoice — money owing.   (2) A statement of — in the case of a receipt — money already paid.

bill of exchange   This document has three parties: the drawer (creditor), the drawee (debtor) and a payee. It is a written promise, by the *drawee,* to pay the *payee* at a specified future time or by a certain date, an amount owing. The document is prepared by the *drawer* who sends it to the drawee for acceptance and signature, whence the drawer becomes the payee.

bin card   A record card of stock kept in a bin, showing the quantities of stock received and issued. A bin may be any form of container such as a tray, box or shelf space. See illustration on page 12.

bond   A certificate issued usually by a government or large institution as evidence of a loan received. Usually the bond will state the date of repayment and the interest payable.

bonus   (1) An amount, paid to employees, over and above the agreed wages.   (2) An incentive for employees who are paid an extra sum if agreed targets of output or sales are achieved. A salesman can earn a bonus based on sales made; a director can be paid a bonus if the company makes a specific profit.

bonus share   A free share issued by a company to an existing shareholder. The share appears to be free since the shareholder makes no direct payment for it. (In most cases however, the shareholder has contributed to the bonus shares because they can only come from profits that have not been distributed to shareholders.)

book of accounts   A book which keeps accounts, e.g. sales ledger, stock ledger, nominal ledger.

book of original entry   A book in which the first record of transactions is made. Same as **book of first entry, book of prime entry** and **memorandum book.**

bookkeeping   The record of the financial transactions of a business.

bought book   Same as **purchases day book.**

bought day book   same as **purchases day book.**

bought ledger   same as **purchases ledger.**

bounced cheque   See **dishonour**.

bound book   A book which has its pages fastened (or bound) together within a cover, thereby preventing pages from being detached and lost.

branch accounts   A bookkeeping method of recording transactions where a business has one or more branches. The accounts required will depend upon the way in which the business is organised. For example: (a) branches may trade independently of the head office and other branches; (b) branches may sell only goods invoiced to it by head office; (c) branches may deal with overseas customers; (d) branches may be located overseas.

brought down (b/d)   The abbreviation b/d is entered in the folio column of a ledger account, showing that the balance entered has been brought down from above the ruled total. See also **balancing accounts.**

brought forward (b/f)   The total of a page, column, or balance on an account, brought forward from a previous page where it was described as c/f (carried forward).

budget   A predetermined plan of activity. Different activities within a business will each have their own budget, e.g. the *production* budget will define the planned output, the *sales* budget will define the planned sales, the *cash* budget will define the expected receipts and payments. When the plans are expressed in monetary terms the budget is referred to as a *financial* budget.

budgetary control   A system which enables the management of a business to control the financial position by establishing a series of budgets for all the activities to be carried out. The collection, recording and analysis of the actual activities in financial terms, then careful comparison with the planned activities, is an essential part of the system.

budgeting   The preparation of budgets.

bulk discount   See **discount types:** *quantity discount.*

business   A business is a commercial or industrial activity concerned with buying goods, selling goods, making goods, or providing a service.

business document   A written or printed record of an event, activity or transaction relating to a business.

business entity concept   All record-keeping is from the business point of view, as opposed to the owner's point of view. This is in order to measure the profitability or otherwise of an individual business. The owner may have transactions with the business (such as providing capital or drawing out profits) and these are recorded in the same way as transactions with any other person.

business transaction   An agreement or deal made between the business and either a person or another business.

Cc

CA   Member of the Institute of Chartered Accountants of Scotland. See also **Chartered Accountant.**

call (of capital)   A request for an instalment to be paid by shareholders of the capital they have agreed to subscribe.

called-up capital   Shareholders who have been alloted shares can be asked to pay by instalments. The total of the instalments requested in payment of the nominal value is known as the *called-up capital*. Opposite of **uncalled capital.**

capital   The investment by an owner, or owners such as shareholders (in the case of a company), in a business. See also **share capital** and **accumulated fund.**

capital account   The account kept in the books of a business recording its dealing with the owner or owners. See also **share capital account** and **business entity concept.**

capital allowance   The amount of depreciation on an asset that the Inland Revenue will allow to be offset against profits. See also **writing down allowance (WDA)** and **first year allowance (FYA).**

capital employed   A business will use the capital provided by its owner(s) to buy fixed assets and provide working capital. If this capital is insufficient to meet the needs of the business then it will borrow further capital (e.g. from banks) or buy goods on credit. The total amount of capital and other finance used by a business is called the *capital employed*. See also **gross capital employed** and **net capital employed.**

capital expenditure   Money used to buy fixed assets which can be retained for use in the business in order to assist the daily activities, e.g. motor vehicles, premises, office equipment, tools and so on. Such expenditure is of lasting benefit.

capital fund   Same as **accumulated fund.**

capital income   Income arising from a capital transaction, e.g. issue of shares at a premium or profits on the sale of assets.

capital profit   A profit arising from a capital transaction, e.g. profits on share dealings, asset sales or revaluations.

capital receipt   Money received by a business either from a capital source (e.g. owner's capital) or from a capital transaction (e.g. sale of property).

capital reserve   See **reserve types**.

capital types   In the case of a limited company, the term capital needs to be qualified. See **authorised capital; called-up capital; circulating capital; floating capital; issued capital; paid-up capital; subscribed capital; uncalled capital; working capital; capital employed.**

capitalization   (1) The conversion of revenue expenditure into capital expenditure, e.g. wages and materials used in extending a factory would be transferred from expense accounts into the factory buildings account as this represents an increase in the asset value.   (2) The total value of a company as measured by the shareholders' interest.

carriage expenses   Expenses of transporting goods.

carriage inwards   The cost of transporting purchases from the supplier to the business premises. This is usually considered a trading expense.

carriage outwards   The cost of transporting goods sold, to the customer's premises. This is usually considered a selling expense.

carried down (c/d) The abbreviation c/d is entered in the folio column next to the balance. It indicates that this difference should be carried down below the ruled totals. See also **balancing accounts.**

carried forward (c/f) The abbreviation c/f is used to denote a total of a page or column which is carried forward to a subsequent page or column. The total when shown on the subsequent page is brought forward (b/f in the folio column).

cash (1) Notes and coins issued by the government readily available for use. (2) Money or cheques used for immediate purchase.

cash account A record of cash transactions. In practice this includes the receipt of cheques from customers.

cash book The book in which both the cash and bank current account transactions are recorded.

cash budget See **budget.**

cash discount See **discount types.**

cash dispenser card A plastic card which enables the bank account holder to withdraw cash from his or her account by the use of a *cash dispenser machine.* These are located outside banks, thus enabling the account holder to draw cash outside normal banking hours.

cash flow The movement of cash into and out of a business. Cash is received from a variety of sources — sale of goods, capital subscribed by owners, receipts from debtors, sale of assets etc. Payments similarly cover a wide field. See also **discounted cash flow** and **net cash flow.**

cash flow statement A statement which shows the effect of cash flows on the cash and bank balances during the course of a year. The effect is shown by listing profits or losses and the resulting changes in assets and liabilities that may have taken place between the two balance sheet dates.

cash payments   Payments using notes, coins, cheques and credit cards.

cash receipts   Receipts of notes, coins, cheques and customers' payments by credit card.

cash received book   A book, subsidiary to the cash book, which is used to record individual receipts, thereby saving the cash book from being overburdened with detail.

cash sales   Sales made for immediate cash payment.

cash transaction   A business deal involving the immediate transfer of cash.

cashier   The person in a business who receives and records the cash and bank transactions.

catalogue price   The selling price of goods, as listed in the supplier's catalogue or price list. Same as **list price.**

certified accountant   A fellow **(FCCA)** or associate **(ACCA)** of the Chartered Association of Certified Accountants.

charges   (1) Payments made by a business from which it must deduct income tax which is payable to the Inland Revenue, e.g. debenture interest, royalties. (2) Persons who have the right to seize business assets in the event of non-payment of interest or non-payment of a loan are said to have a *charge* on assets. (3) Fees charged for services supplied.

chartered accountant   (1) A fellow **(FCA)** or associate **(ACA)** of the Institute of Chartered Accountants in England and Wales.   (2) A fellow **(FCA)** or associate **(ACA)** of the Institute of Chartered Accountants in Ireland.   (3) A member **(CA)** of the Institute of Chartered Accountants of Scotland.

cheque   A written order to a bank by an account holder, requiring the bank to pay a sum of money to the person named on the order. (A cheque is defined in the Bills of Exchange Act 1882.)

cheque card   A card issued to account holders which acts as proof of identity when the account holder is buying goods by cheque or obtaining cash from a bank. The card guarantees to the seller payment by the bank of a sum up to a stated maximum — usually £50.

cheque clearance   The procedure operated by banks enabling the transfer of funds between them when a cheque is paid in by an account holder.

cheque crossings   See **crossed cheques.**

chronological order   The order in which accounts are entered: i.e. by time and date, the earliest first.

circulating assets   Same as **current assets.**

circulating capital   The total value of current assets which change their form from cash to stock, to debtors and back to cash. In this way the value of these assets circulates.

clock card   The name given to a card which records the employee's times of arrival and departure by insertion into a device which has a time-printing mechanism.

closing entries   Entries that close accounts at the end of a trading period by transfer of (a) opening and closing stocks to the Trading account; (b) income and expenses to the final account; (c) drawings to the capital account; (d) the profit and loss account balance to the capital account.

closing stock   The value of stock on hand at the financial year end date. Stocks include raw materials, components, work in progress and finished goods. The value is either cost value or net realisable value, whichever is the lower.

club accounts A club, society or other non-profit-making organisation is usually required by its constitution to supply its members with a set of accounts at the end of its financial year. The principal account presented is an income and expenditure account which shows whether or not the organisation is receiving sufficient income to pay its expenses. A balance sheet may also be prepared.

code number A number derived from the allowances an employee can offset against his income prepared by the Inland Revenue. This number is used by an employer to calculate the income tax to be deducted from an employee's wages.

coding notice Same as **notice of coding.**

coin and note analysis A detailed record of the quantities of notes and coins required to be withdrawn from the bank to meet specific requirements, e.g. making up wage packets. See illustration below.

Coin and Note Analysis Sheet

NOTE AND COIN ANALYSIS		B. MADDISON LIMITED		Week No: 8 Week Ending: 30th May									
Employee	Net Wage	£50	£20	£10	£5	£2	£1	50p	20p	10p	5p	2p	1p
T. Black	142·50	2	2			1		1					
S. Gold	198·35	3	2			1	1	1		1	1	1	
A. Robb	168·90	3		1	1	1	1	1	2				
M. Starr	155·66	3			1			1		1	1		1
F. Wood	187·82	3	1	1	1	1		1	1	1		1	
	853·23	14	5	2	4	4	2	4	4	3	2	1	1

columnar book   Same as **analysed book.**

commission   Fees and charges for services performed. Commissions received are the charges made by a business for its services; they may be based on a percentage of turnover of the customer's business. See also **bank charges**.

commission (error of)   See **error of commission.**

company (limited)   The name given to an enterprise which has a legal personality in its own right independent of its members (who are the owners). See also **limited company** and **public limited company.**

company accounts   (1) The accounts of a company.   (2) Accounts which are required by the Companies Act to be presented to shareholders are referred to as *published accounts.*

Companies Act   The rules and requirements laid down by Parliament to control the formation and operation of limited companies. All the previous Acts were consolidated in the 1985 Companies Act.

compensating error   See **error of compensation.**

complementary arithmetic   A method of calculating a figure by adding the sum necessary to complete the whole rather than by using subtraction.

compulsory winding up   Winding-up is the legal term for closing down a business. A compulsory winding-up is the closing down of a business by the court. There are several circumstances arising in which the court would, if petitioned by either the company itself or any creditor or contributory, wind up a company. The most common circumstance is where a business is unable to pay its debts.

computer hardware   All the electronic and mechanical elements of a computer and the devices used in a computer system, e.g. visual display unit **(VDU),** central processing unit **(CPU),** printer, disk drive, keyboard,

computer software   A general term describing programs which can be used in computer systems. These are divided into applications software and system software. See also **package.**

computerised accounting   The recording, collecting and analysis of the financial transactions of a business using computer equipment.

concept of accounting   An idea which accountants believe, in general, should guide the action taken in dealing with particular aspects of accounting. See **business entity concept; consistency concept; cost concept; dual aspect concept; going concern concept; matching concept; materiality concept; money measurement concept; prudence concept; realisation concept.**

conservatism concept   Same as **prudence concept.**

consignment accounts   The records kept by a business sending goods to an agent for sale on commission. The goods remain the property of the business until sold.

consignment note   Same as **delivery note.**

consistency concept   Having selected methods of dealing with certain aspects of accounting, it is expected that the methods will be used in future periods. Consistency enables the proper comparisons to be made between accounting figures of different periods. If methods are altered to satisfy the business interests at different times, comparison becomes difficult. (If a change does become necessary then a note should be made in the accounts.)

consolidated accounts   Where a company holds more than 50% of another (subsidiary) company then it is described as a holding company. Holding companies and subsidiary companies together form a group and the Companies Act requires consolidated (or group) accounts to be presented to shareholders. The consolidated accounts include a profit and loss account and a balance sheet.

container A crate, carton, carboy, reel, barrel, packet, box, tin, etc., which is used to hold or transport products. Some containers may be considered a cost of the product (e.g. crisp packets) whilst others may be charged to customers with refunds if returned. This term also describes the large lorry-size box used to transport goods over long distances by road.

container accounts The accounting procedure for containers. In the case of returnable or refundable containers, it is necessary to ensure that adequate stock records are kept and the amounts refundable properly recorded.

contingency A possible future event which is considered unlikely to occur.

contingent liability A loss that may arise in the future, dependent upon the outcome of transactions already undertaken. To cover the possibility of losses, a note is attached to the balance sheet detailing the amounts. (If the loss was expected, then a provision would be made.)

continuous balance A balance which is computed and shown after each transaction on an account. This is commonplace in mechanised and computerised accounts using the three column account form. Customer statements are usually presented showing a continuous balance. Same as **running balance**.

continuous inventory A stock control system and stock ledger system which maintains an accurate and up-to-date list of stock items and their values.

contra entries These entries arise in the cashbook when cash is paid into or drawn out of the bank. Since the double-entry recording of such an event is in the same book, the letter C is shown in the folio column.

contract accounts   A system of recording and allocating costs and income in such a way that the profit or loss made on individual contracts can be determined even when not fully completed. Often used by companies in the building construction and civil engineering industry.

contribution   The amount contributed by a product towards the payment of the fixed costs of the business. It is measured by deducting the variable cost of the product from the selling price.

control account   An account which summarises the entries and balances in the ledger. The amounts debited and credited to the control accounts represent the total of the entries made in individual accounts in the ledgers. This account is not a part of the double entry system. A control account is more correctly called a **total account**.

conventions   The established view of accountants in general, and of the rules to be followed in carrying out practices and concepts. Same as **accounting conventions**. See also **concept of accounting** and **statement of standard accounting practice**.

copyright   The exclusive right of the author or composer of literary or artistic work, to use that work. Such rights can be sold. See also **patent rights.**

corporation tax   The tax levied on the profits of limited companies.

correcting entries   Since the deletion or erasure of entries is not good accounting practice, errors are corrected by making further entries to amend the accounts. Correcting entries are made in ledger accounts, the journal being used as the book of original entry in which each error and its correction is explained.

correction of errors   Errors that arise in a bookkeeping system need to be corrected by means of additional entries.

cost   (1) The amount of money paid for a product or service. Also called **expenditure.**   (2) To 'cost a job' means to work out how much the job or contract will cost. This cost will then be used as the basis of the selling price.

cost and management accountant   A fellow (**FCMA**) or associate (**ACMA**) of the Institute of Cost and Management Accountants.

cost concept   Valuing assets is difficult since their values vary as time passes. Some increase and most decrease and this may be according to opinion. The cost concept means showing the historic cost price of assets in the annual accounts, thereby providing an unquestionable basis for comparison and measurement based on the investment made in them.

cost of goods sold   The cost price of the goods that have been sold. The figure is shown in the trading account and is calculated as follows:
cost of goods sold = opening stock + purchases − closing stock.
This cost, deducted from the sales, leaves gross profit.

cost of manufactured goods   Same as **production cost**.

cost of production   Same as **production cost**.

cost of sales   Same as **cost of goods sold**.

cost of stock sold   Same as **cost of goods sold**.

cost price   The price paid by a person or business for a product or service supplied.

CPU (of computer)   Central Processing Unit. That part of a computer system in which the program instructions are stored and processed (carried out).

credit   (1) 'To credit' means to make a credit entry. (2) 'In credit' reflects the state of a person's bank account as shown by the bank statement. It is in credit when money exists in the account, i.e. when there is a credit balance from the point of view of the bank.

credit balance   The balance on an account which results from credit entries exceeding the debit entries.

credit card   A card which allows the holder to buy goods or services without paying cash at that time. The card holder usually signs a voucher which is then imprinted with his or her name and that of the issuing company who will pay the bill. The holder will later settle his or her bill with the credit card company.

credit control   The system used by a business to ensure that new credit customers are acceptable and that existing customers do not exceed the agreed maximum figure and pay on the due date.

credit customer   A customer who is allowed to purchase goods and pay for them at a later time.

credit entry   A credit entry is shown on the right-hand side of an account. This indicates value given. For example, when payment is received from a debtor the value given by the debtor is recorded on the credit side of the debtor's account. Another example is sales. When goods are sold, the business has 'given' their value.

credit limit   The maximum amount, in terms of value, that a customer can have outstanding on his or her account.

credit note   A document, often printed in red, sent to a customer showing that the customer's account has been credited with the amount shown. This arises for example when a customer: (a) has returned goods; (b) has been overcharged; (c) is refunded for containers returned; (d) is given an allowance for damaged goods.

credit period   The amount of time allowed to a credit customer before payment is expected.

credit sales   Sales made to a customer who will pay at a later time.

credit transaction   A business deal which does not involve the immediate payment of cash but requires settlement at a later time.

credit transfer   (1) A method of settling bills whereby a person or business can pay a sum of money into any account at any bank. The cash can be handed into any bank provided it is accompanied by a bank giro credit slip of that bank.   (2) Paying a number of amounts or bills by the use of the one cheque (often used for salary payments).

creditor   A person or business to whom money is owed.

creditors' ledger   Same as **purchases ledger**.

creditors' voluntary winding up   Where a company itself decides to wind up, it can be either a creditors' voluntary winding up or a members' voluntary winding up. The creditors' voluntary winding up takes place where the directors' statutory declaration has not been made. This form of winding up requires the creditors to appoint a liquidator who winds up the affairs of the company and distributes assets to creditors.

creditworthiness   A term used by a business when deciding the ability or willingness of a customer to pay his bills.

cross-casting   Totalling a set of figures that are written horizontally (rather than in a list). Often used as a check of arithmetic in analysed books.

crossed cheque   Two parallel lines drawn across the face of a cheque mean that the cheque is crossed and may only be cleared by payment into a bank account. Various words can be inserted between the lines which restrict the transfer of the cheque. These include:

(a) *Not negotiable*, whilst not preventing the cheque from being passed on, does not necessarily confer good title (i.e. a guarantee of payment) to subsequent holders.

(b) *Account payee* means that a cheque would normally only be paid into the account of the payee. Special authorisation is required for transfer to another person.

Special crossing restricts a cheque's free transfer. For example, if the name of a bank and branch are written between the two lines, then the paying bank will only transfer funds to the account held at the branch of that bank.

cum div   All prices of shares quoted on the stock exchange are cum div unless expressly stated to be ex div. The term *cum div* means including dividend. When shares are purchased, the purchaser will receive the next dividend to be paid by the company.

cumulative preference share   See **preference share**.

current account   A bank account which enables the account holder to take out money at any time and also to make payment to other people using cheques.

current assets   These are assets which continually change as business transactions take place, e.g. cash, stock, debtors and bank balances. Same as **circulating assets**.

current cost   A value which represents the present-day value of an asset, liability, income or expense calculated from an historic cost which has been adjusted by the appropriate index number to allow for inflation.

current cost accounting   The accounting procedures that convert final accounts and balance sheets prepared on the normal historic cost basis to current costs.

current liability   See **liability types**.

current ratio   Same as **working capital ratio**.

cut-off   The 'cut-off point' is the point in time at which specific actions are taken (or cease) in order to ensure agreement exists between different sections of the business. Cut-off procedures are essential in end-of-year accounting. For example, with regard to closing stock valuation, materials purchased but not received are included while goods sold but not despatched are excluded.

Dd

data All basic facts such as amounts, names and dates.

data base Files of data stored on computer media. Such data is independent of application programs but can be used as required with an appropriate program.

data capture The procedure for converting data into a form which can be processed by a computer.

data control The recording and monitoring of data being entered into or already within or being produced by a computer, to ensure its correct processing.

data processing A general term covering the procedures involved in collecting, sorting, recording, analysing, interpreting and storing information.

day book Same as **book of original entry**.

debenture A long-term loan evidenced by the issue of a certificate. Occasionally it is a loan made at a fixed rate of interest which is unsecured. This means that, should the borrower go out of business, the debenture holder will not be able to take over assets if loan repayments or interest repayments are not made. See also **secured debenture** and **floating debenture**.

debit (1) A debit entry in an account is referred to as a debit. (2) To debit, means to make a debit entry.

debit balance The balance on an account which results from debit entries exceeding the credit entries.

debit entry A debit entry is shown on the left hand side of an account. The entry shows value received. For example, cash received is debited in the cash account. Another example is wages and salaries. The business has received the value of employees' services.

debit note   A document sent to a customer showing that the customer's account has been debited with the amount shown. Usually used to adjust invoices or act as a supplementary invoice.

debt   (1) An amount owed by one person to another.   (2) 'In debt' is the condition of a person who owes money. See also **liability**.

debtor   A person or business who owes money.

debtors' ledger   Same as **sales ledger**.

declining balance method   See **depreciation methods: reducing balance**.

deductions from pay   Amounts that an employer will deduct from the gross pay of employees. See also **statutory deductions** and **voluntary deductions.**

deed of partnership   Same as **partnership deed**.

deficiency   The amount by which the annual income of a non-profit-making organisation falls short of the annual expenditure.

del credere commission   An additional commission paid to an agent for agreeing to reimburse his or her principal for losses arising from debtors who fail to pay their debts.

delivery note   A document completed by the seller of goods, providing written details of the goods and attached to them, giving the address to which delivery is to be made.

departmental account   An account recording the transactions and trading results of a department within an organisation — such as departments within large stores.

depletion unit method   See **depreciation methods :** *depletion unit.*

deposit account   A bank account usually used for savings because interest is paid by the bank on the amount deposited. Prior notice may be required for the withdrawal of money. See also **bank pass book**.

depreciation   The loss in the value of assets due to wear and tear, obsolescence or passage of time.

depreciation fund account   Same as **sinking fund account**.

depreciation fund investment account   Same as **sinking fund investment account**.

depreciation methods

(a)   *depletion unit*   A method used with mines and quarries. The estimated tonnage expected to be extracted during useful life is divided into the total cost to obtain a rate per unit. The depreciation is the actual content extracted multiplied by the rate.

(b)   *machine hour*   The total machine running hours during useful life are estimated and divided into the cost. This machine hour rate is then applied to the actual running hours in each year to calculate the depreciation.

(c)   *reducing balance*   An agreed fixed percentage rate is predetermined and this is applied to the written down value of the asset at the beginning of each year (i.e. the reduced value). Same as **declining balance** or **diminishing balance method**.

(d)   *revaluation depreciation*   Assets are revalued each year and the amount of depreciation is therefore calculated as the difference between the yearly valuations. This method is often used for fixed assets which are dispersed throughout the business and are of low cost, e.g. hand tools.

(e)   *straight line*   The original cost value is reduced each year by an agreed and fixed percentage of that cost. Same as **fixed instalment** and **equal instalment methods**.

(f)   *sum of the digits*   A reducing balance method in which the life in years is converted to units or digits. This is done by allocating to each year the same number of digits as the estimated life left. For example, a new asset with three years life will have $3+2+1=6$ digits.

The first year's depreciation will equal 3/6 of the cost, the second year 2/6 of cost, and the last year 1/6 of cost.

diminishing balance method   See **depreciation methods:** *reducing balance*.

direct cost   A cost that can be measured and identified as being incurred on a specific job, contract or process. Such costs vary in direct proportion to output, increasing as output rises and falling as output diminishes.

direct debit   A method whereby a bank account holder can arrange to pay regular or frequent sums without writing a cheque. The account holder authorises his bank to accept demands for payments made by the payee. Unlike a standing order, which requires the payer to authorise changes, a direct debit authorisation enables the payee to vary his demands.

direct expenses   These are direct costs other than direct labour and direct material.

direct labour   This is a direct cost, being the labour costs of the employees whose time on the manufacture of specified products can be measured. The direct labour cost can therefore be allocated directly to the goods being produced. Same as **direct wages**.

direct material   This is a direct cost, being the material used in the manufacture of specified products.

direct wages   Same as **direct labour**.

director   A person appointed by the shareholders of a limited company to direct its affairs on their behalf. As an officer of the company, a director is responsible for ensuring that the company meets the obligations imposed upon it by company law.

directors' remuneration   Salaries, fees and other benefits paid to directors by the company employing them.

directors' report   The annual report of the directors of a company which has to be included as a part of the information given to shareholders (as required by the Companies Act).

discount   A reduction in the selling price of goods.

discount allowed   Discount allowed to customers who fulfil certain conditions.

discount disallowed   Where a discount has been previously allowed to a customer and is now disallowed. For example, when a discount is given for prompt payment but the cheque paid is then dishonoured, the debtor must revert to the original position and thus the discount is now disallowed.

discount period   The time allowed for a debtor to pay his or her bill and claim the discount offered. Often specified periods are shown on the bill.

discount received   Discount received from suppliers.

discount types   (a) *cash discount*   A reduction in the price of goods because of the buyer's immediate or prompt payment.   (b) *quantity discount*   A reduction in the unit price of goods given when large quantities are purchased. Same as **bulk discount**.   (c) *trade discount*   A reduction in the catalogue price of goods given by one trader to another. See also **allowances**.

discounted cash flow   The present value of future estimated cash flows.

discounting   The process of calculating the present value of a sum to be received in the future.

discounting bills of exchange   Receiving from a bank the money value of a bill of exchange before the bill reaches maturity (i.e. the due date for payment). The bank holds the bill until maturity and it is then reimbursed by the acceptor of the bill. For this service the bank makes a discounting charge.

discounting charge   See **discounting bills of exchange**.

dishonour   Failure of a debtor to make good his or her promise to pay — e.g. dishonour of a cheque and dishonour of a bill of exchange as when a cheque presented to a bank for payment is returned to the payee as no funds are available to pay the sum due. The bank will mark the cheque *no funds — refer to drawer* (abbreviated **R/D**).

disk   See **media**.

disposal of assets   When assets are no longer required, they can be sold, exchanged, or scrapped. Such physical disposals will need a corresponding bookkeeping entry to remove the value of the assets from the accounts.

dividend   Money paid to a shareholder as a return on investment. Dividends are paid out of profits and are expressed as a percentage of the nominal value of the share. Interim dividends may be paid — these are usually based on half-year profits.

dividend warrant   This is a cheque paying a dividend to a shareholder.

dividend yield ratio   The dividend received by a shareholder, measured as a percentage of the market price of his or her shares.

division of the ledger   The ledger is the main book of account and in a large firm it will need to be divided into separate sections (or books) in which similar groups of accounts are kept together. The usual divisions are: **asset ledger**; **nominal ledger**; **private ledger**; **purchases ledger**; **sales ledger**; **stock ledger**. See separate entries.

documents   Papers, records, booklets, sheets which provide data or enable data to be recorded.

double entry   The system of bookkeeping which requires each transaction to be recorded twice. A payment, for example, is only made because services or goods have been received. In double entry bookkeeping the receiving and giving (payment) aspects are both recorded, each in a different account.

DP   Abbreviation for **data processing**.

drawee   (1) The bank from whom payment will be required when an account holder draws a cheque.   (2) The business or person specified in a **bill of exchange** as the party that is to pay the sum stated on the bill. This is usually the debtor of the drawer.

drawer   (1) The drawer of a cheque is the bank account holder who signs the cheque. The term *drawer* comes from the 'drawing up' of a cheque which means completing the details necessary to ensure it becomes a valid order. (2)The originator of a **bill of exchange**, i.e. the person who prepares the bill and sends it to the drawee. The drawer is frequently the payee, i.e. the person to whom payment is to be made.

drawings   The owner of a business is entitled to take out of the business profits due to him or her, and also to take out stock, assets or make private payments through the business bank accounts. Any monies or other assets taken by the owner, or paid by the business on his or her behalf, are called *drawings*.

dual aspect concept   This concept concerns the principle of double entry. The basis being that each transaction has two aspects and each aspect has to be recorded. See also **concept of accounting** and **double entry**.

due date   (1) The date by which a payment is required to be made.   (2) The date on which a payment falls due.

Ee

E & OE   Abbreviation for *errors and omissions excepted*. This abbreviation often appears on invoices and means that, if the supplier has made any errors on the invoice, the details can be altered to the correct ones.

earnings per share   The available net profit after tax measured as a percentage of the nominal share capital issued. This gives a measure of how much the shareholders would have received had the directors recommended all the profit to be paid out as dividends.

embezzlement   Using someone else's money or property for one's own purposes without the knowledge and agreement of the owner.

employed capital   Same as **capital employed.**

endorsement of cheque   To endorse a cheque means (the payee) to sign the back of the cheque. This indicates that the payee has 'received' the value of the cheque by passing the cheque to another person.

equal instalment method   See **depreciation methods:** *straight line*.

equity finance   Same as **equity share capital.**

equity share capital   Capital subscribed by ordinary shareholders.

error of commission   This is an error of misposting, where an entry is posted to the wrong account within the same class of account. An example would be if *motor* expenses are posted to the *insurance* account, which are both expense accounts.

error of compensation   If several errors arise, it is possible for the effects not to be shown because the books still balance. For example, the same over-calculation could arise on both the debit side of an account and the credit side of another account. Same as **compensating error.**

error of misposting   An error made in posting an entry to the wrong account. The correct side of the account has been entered, but the entry has been made in the wrong account. See also **error of commission** and **error of principle.**

error of omission   If a transaction is omitted from the book of original entry then it will neither be debited nor credited. Consequently, whilst the books balance, the accounts are incorrect.

error of original entry   Where an incorrect figure is entered in a book of original entry, this will cause the same wrong figure to be entered in the ledger accounts.

error of principle   This is an error of misposting but of a more serious nature than an error of commission. This occurs when an entry is posted to the wrong class of account. It usually arises because of confusion between *revenue* and *capital* items. For example, motor expenses should appear in the motor expenses account. If erroneously posted to the motor vehicle account, the books still balance, but the asset account is overstated and the expense account understated.

error of reversal   Where a transaction is entered on the wrong side of the two accounts then an error of reversal has occurred. This often arises when an entry has been made on the wrong side of the cash or bank account in the cash book.

error of transposition   This is the writing down of a value or number in which two or more figures are in the wrong order, e.g. writing £693 instead of £639.

ex div   This term means excluding dividend. *Ex div* refers to the purchase of stocks or shares, and means that the seller and not the purchaser is entitled to the next payment of interest or dividends.

exchange rates   These rates are those established in the Foreign Exchange market where foreign currencies are bought and sold.

exempt rating (VAT)   A business, supplying goods or services that are classed as exempt supplies by the VAT legislation, is given an *exempt rating* by H.M. Customs and Excise. This means that the business does not add VAT to the price charged for its goods or services, neither is the business able to reclaim VAT paid on its expenses. See also **zero rating (VAT)**.

exempt supplies   Goods or services supplied by a business which do not require the business to charge VAT.

expenditure   Same as **cost**.

expense accounts   Accounts in the **nominal ledger** recording the revenue expenditure incurred on goods bought for resale and services supplied to the business, e.g. wages, rent, insurance, advertising etc.

expense types   (a) Capital expense. (b) Revenue expense. See **capital** and **revenue expenditure**.

expenses outstanding   Same as **accrual**.

expenses owing   Same as **accrual**.

exposure draft   A proposal, issued by accountancy bodies, requesting responses from members. The proposal usually deals with an accountancy matter and if there is a general consensus of opinion the exposure draft could lead to the issue of a **statement of standard accountancy practice (SSAP)** or an **international accounting standard**.

external liability   See **liability types**.

extraordinary item   An unusual gain or loss which arises from an event or transaction not within the normal activities of the business. The gain or loss is material and would not be expected to occur frequently.

ex-works price   Where a price is quoted as *ex-works*, the cost of moving the goods beyond the supplier's factory gates is the responsibility of the buyer.

Ff

face value   The value shown on the face of a coin, note or share certificate. See also **nominal value**.

factoring   This is the process intended to : (a) provide immediate payment from debtors; (b) save the administrative cost of debt collection. When an invoice is sent to a customer, the *factoring agent* (if used by a company) will pay the invoice total (less a commission charge) to the company. The agent then takes over the sales ledger recording and collection of the amount owed by the debtor.

factory cost   Same as **production cost**.

factory expenses   Same as **production cost**.

factory overheads   Same as **production overheads**.

FCA   (1) Fellow of the Institute of Chartered Accountants in England and Wales.   (2) Fellow of the Institute of Chartered Accountants in Ireland. See **chartered accountant**.

FCCA   Fellow of the Chartered Association of Certified Accountants. See **certified accountant**.

FCMA   Fellow of the Institute of Cost and Management Accountants. See **cost and management accountant**.

feasibility study   Where a major change in any aspect of an organisation is intended, it is sensible to carry out a detailed study. All the implications including probable benefits and disadvantages need to be considered before implementation of any proposals. For example, changing from manual to computerised bookkeeping or introducing a new product line in the factory.

fictitious asset   Expenses incurred but not written off to the profit and loss account. Although no asset exists the balance carried forward is shown in the balance sheet. This may occur where some benefit from the expenses may be considered to arise in the future, e.g. advertising expenses.

fidelity bond   An insurance policy that protects employers from losses incurred by the dishonesty of employees.

FIFO   Abbreviation for **first in first out**. See **pricing methods**.

final accounts   Company law requires directors to prepare year-end accounts for shareholders showing the results of the company activities. The Inland Revenue wish to know the profit or loss of all businesses. Both of these requirements are met by the preparation of annual final accounts which are prepared to show the financial results of the business. The final accounts are different according to the type of business: (a) for a trading company, they are the **trading** and **profit and loss accounts**; (b) for a service business, it is a **revenue account**; (c) for a manufacturing business, they are the **manufacturing**, **trading** and **profit and loss accounts**. If the business is a partnership or limited company an additional account is required, called the **appropriation account**. (A balance sheet always accompanies the final accounts because this statement shows the assets and liabilities of the business at the year end date.)

finance cost   The cost of obtaining and using borrowed finance, e.g. bank interest charges, hire purchase interest, arrangement fees.

finance lease   See **lease types**.

financial accountant   An accountant who is concerned with the financial recording and preparation of the final accounts.

financial accounting   The work of a financial accountant.

financial budget   See **budget**.

financial event   Any event that has a financial implication for the business. It could be, for example, a normal transaction or an unusual occurrence such as an earthquake that destroys the business assets.

financial period   Same as **accounting period**.

financial statement   Any statement which portrays financial affairs can be called a financial statement, e.g. a budget, a profit and loss account, a balance sheet.

financial transaction   A deal, agreement, or bargain between persons or companies which involves the exchange of money.

financial year   The twelve-month period of a business whose financial activities are summarised by the final accounts.

financial year end   The date on which the year ends for the purposes of preparation of the final accounts.

first in first out (FIFO)   See **pricing methods**.

first year allowance (FYA)   A term used by the Inland Revenue to describe the amount of depreciation (**capital allowance**) they will allow at the end of the financial year in which an asset was purchased. See also **writing down allowance**.

fiscal period   In taxation law, this is the year ending on 5th April in each year. Otherwise same as **accounting period**.

fixed asset utilisation ratio   Same as **sales to fixed assets ratio**.

fixed assets   Assets that are used over a period of time in a business to enable the business to earn profit. Examples are machinery in a factory, ships of a shipping company, office equipment. See also **intangible** and **tangible assets**.

fixed capital   (1) The value of fixed assets.   (2) Capital contributed by partners which will not be withdrawn or altered without agreement of the partners.

fixed cost   An expense which does not vary with the level of activity of the business and is incurred irrespective of the activity achieved. For example, business rates and interest on loans have to be paid whether or not the business is operating.

fixed debenture   Same as **secured debenture**.

fixed expense   Same as **fixed cost**.

fixed instalment method   See **depreciation methods** : *straight line*.

flexible budget   This is a set of budgets. Each individual budget is prepared for different levels of activity or output. The actual cost can then be compared with the budgeted costs at the level of activity achieved so that efficiency can be properly measured.

floating capital   Same as **circulating capital**.

floating debenture   A loan made to a company which gives the debenture holders the right to appoint a receiver to take over assets if loan repayments or interest payments are not made and then to run the company in the interests of the debenture holders. Where all of the assets are charged by debenture holders, the debentures are said to 'float' over the assets. See also **secured debentures**.

floppy disk   See **media**.

flow of funds statement   A statement showing the sources from which money has been received by a business and the uses made of that money by the business.

folio column   The column in both books and accounts in which the folio reference is recorded. See illustration on page 47.

folio reference   The identifying reference of the account to which an entry has been posted, or the book of original entry from which a posting has been made. This reference is entered in the folio column of accounts and books.

forfeited shares   Shares which have been cancelled by a company because a shareholder has failed to pay the money (calls) requested in payment for the shares.

formation expenses   Same as **preliminary expenses**.

free pay   The amount of income an employee receives before paying income tax. See also **code number** and **taxable pay**.

free stock   Stock either on hand or on order, which has not been allocated for use or sale. Such stock is available to meet any future requirement.

freehold   The description which is given to land and/or buildings which are owned in perpetuity.

fund   A store, supply or source of money.

fundamental accounting principle   A basic rule of accounting. See also **SSAP, conventions** and **concept of accounting**.

funds flow   Same as **cash flow**.

funds flow statement   Same as **flow of funds statement**.

FYA   Abbreviation for **first year allowance**.

Gg

gearing   The relationship between the capital invested by the owner(s) and the funds borrowed, e.g. loans and debentures which are usually referred to as loan capital. The purpose of measuring this relationship is to show how much the business depends on borrowed money in comparison with the owner's money.

gearing ratio   The ratio of loan capital to owner's investment. A low-geared business has a small proportion of borrowed money whilst a highly-geared business has a greater proportion of borrowed money than owner's money. In a highly-geared business fluctuations in owner's return are more likely to occur. Also suppliers of loan capital may have an influence on running the business.

general journal   Same as **journal proper**.

general ledger   A book which contains nominal accounts. In a small business which does not keep a separate *private ledger* or *asset ledger*, then the general ledger will also contain private accounts and asset accounts. See illustration on page 47.

general reserve   Profits which have been set aside for retention in the business but not for any specified purpose. As a revenue reserve, it can be used for any purpose and would normally be used to cover unexpected losses.

going concern concept   This concept requires the accounts to reflect the state of a business which is expected to carry on trading in future years (i.e. a going concern). If it is known that the business is not going to continue, for any reason, then to be true and fair, the accounts must show instead the assets of their current saleable value.

General Ledger Layout
General Ledger of B. Maddison M2
Motor Expenses Account of B. Maddison

Date	Details	Folio	£ p	Date	Details	Folio	£ p
19-9	Total	b/f	1811·61				
May 31	Petrol	CB26	52·17				
June 30	Petrol	CB30	61·67				
July 4	Insurance	CB31	103·92				
July 14	R.F.L.	J18	120·00				
July 31	Petrol	CB36	70·63	July 31	Revenue Account		2220·00
			2220·00				2220·00
Aug. 30	Petrol	CB40	91·62				
		c/f				c/f	

Folio references refer to the page number in the book of original entry from which this entry is posted — CB is Cash Book, J is Journal.

Abbreviations: b/f=Brought forward
c/f=Carried forward
See Journal layout (page 57) for source of July 4 entry

goods for own use   Stock taken by the owner for his or her own private purposes. For bookkeeping purposes, the sale price of the goods taken is debited to the owner's drawings account and credited to the sales account. In this way the goods are sold to the owner. An alternative is to debit drawings with the cost price of the goods and debit this to the purchases account.

goods received note   A document completed by the storekeeper upon receipt of materials or goods from an outside supplier. When payment is made for the goods, the note is evidence of the quantity of goods received.

goodwill An intangible asset that represents the value to a business of its existing trade and reputation. For example, by providing an efficient service or sound products, a business will have built up a reputation and regular customers. This established trade would be part of the business assets if sold. Its value is the amount a purchaser actually pays for it.

gross capital employed The capital and other finance used by a business, which is the total value of assets as shown on the balance sheet. This value is sometimes used to measure the return on capital.

gross earnings A person's total income received from all sources.

gross loss The loss made when the cost of goods exceeds their sales value.

gross profit The profit made on the sale of goods, being the difference between the cost price of the goods sold and the sales price obtained.

gross profit margin This is the gross profit expressed as a percentage of sales. It is calculated as follows:

$$\text{gross profit margin} = \frac{\text{gross profit} \times 100\%}{\text{sales}}$$

This is one of the measures used to compare the results with previous results.

gross profit mark-up This is the gross profit expressed as a percentage of the cost price of goods (*buying price*). It is calculated as follows:

$$\text{gross profit mark-up} = \frac{\text{gross profit} \times 100\%}{\text{cost of goods sold}}$$

Related to the gross profit margin (but always a higher figure), this percentage is used to measure the performance of the business. In a trading business it shows the average percentage of the cost price of goods that is added to the cost price for profits.

Hh

handwritten accounting books   Books of original entry and ledgers recording the financial affairs of the business which are entered by hand. Many small businesses use handwritten accounting books, as more sophisticated systems are unnecessary and are not worthwhile in terms of cost benefits. Most larger companies enter the same data into computerised systems.

hard disk   See **media**.

hire purchase   An arrangement whereby the owner of goods hires them to a person (the *hirer*) on condition that the hirer pays a certain number of instalments to the owner. The ownership passes to the hirer on payment of the final instalment unless the agreement specifies otherwise.

historic cost   The actual price paid. All accounts are based on historic cost unless otherwise indicated. (Where accounts are prepared to show the effect of inflation, then current costs are quoted.)

historic cost convention   Same as **cost concept**.

holding company   A company which has a majority (i.e. controlling) shareholding in another company. The holding company can dictate the affairs of its subsidiary companies.

horizontal presentation   The layout of a statement across the page. Horizontal presentation usually refers to the layout of a balance sheet which shows assets on the left side and liabilities on the right side. See also **vertical presentation**.

HP   Abbreviation for **hire purchase**.

Ii

impersonal accounts A general name for nominal accounts, asset accounts and any other accounts recording transactions not related to persons.

impersonal ledger Same as **general ledger**.

imprest amount Where the imprest system operates, this is the amount of cash reimbursed to the cashier to restore his cash balance to the float amount. The sum reimbursed is the exact sum paid out during a pre-arranged period.

imprest system A method of keeping and recording the petty cash in which the cashier is given a fixed amount, usually called the *float*. Petty cash is paid out as required or may be paid in. At regular intervals the float is reimbursed with the sum spent, which restores the cash balance to the agreed amount.

income (1) Earnings from supplying goods and/or services and the sale of capital items. See also **revenue income** and **capital income**. (2) The amount of money received by an individual from earned and unearned sources.

income accounts Nominal accounts recording the value of earnings, e.g. rents received, fees/commissions received, discount received.

income and expenditure account The final account of a non-profit making organisation which shows the income and expenditure for the financial year, enabling its members to see whether the income exceeds expenditure (a *surplus*) or vice versa (a *deficiency*). This account is the non-profit-making organisation's equivalent to a trading company's profit and loss account. This account is presented to members at the annual general meeting with a balance sheet.

income tax   A contribution to the State by individuals, based on each person's income. For employees, a deduction is made by the employer from the employee's earnings. The amount paid by each person will vary since allowances are given to individuals according to their personal circumstances. Gross income less allowance is called *taxable income* and this is then taxed at the rates determined by the annual Finance Acts.

incomplete records   Business records which may or may not show the details of all transactions. Such records require the double entry to be completed and may require estimated figures to complete the final accounts. For example, if the owner's drawings are not fully recorded, then drawings are estimated as the difference between the cash received and the cash remaining after paying expenses.

incorporation   The process of forming and legally registering an organisation as a limited company.

index number   A number which shows the change-over time that has occurred in a price, quantity or value in comparison to the value in a previously agreed base period. The value in the base period is usually given the figure 100. For example, the *Retail Price Index* (RPI) shows the increase (or decrease) in the prices of essential household goods consumed by the (average) family. If the current RPI is 150 then it will show that prices have increased by 50% compared with the base period.

indirect expenses   Same as **overhead costs**.

indirect labour   The cost of those employees in a business other than direct labour. It will include storekeepers, maintenance men, administrative staff, sales staff, designers, truck drivers and so on.

inflation   The part of the increase in the price of goods and services which is caused by the decrease in purchasing power of money.

inflation accounting   A method of presenting the results of a business which attempts to show the historical results adjusted for the declining value of money. The usual accounts presented are based on historic cost and objective investment. Assets however, both current and fixed, will need to be replaced on the basis of present day values and not original costs.

Inland Revenue   The Civil Service department that deals with the national arrangements for implementing and carrying out the statutory legislation on income tax, corporation tax, capital gains tax, capital transfer tax and land development tax. Two branches exist:
(a) *Her Majesty's Inspectors* who deal with individuals and companies in determining the income to be assessed for tax.
(b) *Collectors* who collect the amount determined by the Inspectors.

insolvency   The situation that exists where a debtor is unable to pay his or her debts as and when they become due. An insolvent person is not automatically a bankrupt, as bankruptcy depends upon a court ruling.

insurance   A method of protecting a business or individual against losses that arise from known possible risks such as accidents, theft, fire. Purchase of the relevant insurance policies ensures that minimum financial losses are incurred where an insured event arises, through payments by the insurance company.

intangible asset   An asset which exists but cannot be physically seen. Examples are goodwill, patents and copyrights. Intangible assets are shown on the balance sheet as the first item on the asset side under the heading of *fixed assets*.

integrated accounting system   (1) A system in which the prime records and financial accounts are recorded in such a way that they serve as the basis for both the financial accounts and the cost accounts. In this way a completely separate cost accounting system is avoided. (Where separate systems exist, it is necessary to reconcile the profits as disclosed in the financial accounting system with the total of the 'profit' made by individual products as shown by the cost accounting system.) (2) A computerised accounting system in which all the ledgers are linked. Thus a sales invoice will automatically be recorded in the sales ledger, the sales day book and the sales ledger control account, and will be available for trial balance and final account preparation.

interest A person who lends money expects to receive some reward. The charge made to the borrower is the reward and is called *interest*. For example, banks borrow money from depositors and pay them interest.

interest on capital Payments made to partners (out of profits) to reward them for investing capital in the business. Such interest is agreed at a fixed rate by the partners and is intended to replace the interest that partners would obtain if they invested their capital outside the partnership business.

interest on debentures Debenture holders have lent money to a business, and their interest is the money they are entitled to receive from the business as a payment for the use of the money borrowed from them.

interest on drawings A charge made by a partnership business for money withdrawn by partners. (This is not a common practice and often applies only when a partner has drawn sums in excess of previously agreed amounts.)

inter-firm comparison The use of data supplied by a number of companies in the same industry to provide statistics enabling comparisons of efficiency ratios and measures to be made.

interim dividends Dividends paid by a company to shareholders during the course of a financial year before the final accounts have been prepared.

interim final accounts   Final accounts prepared for a period of time less than the financial year (e.g. quarterly or half-yearly) which are used to measure the performance of the business, e.g. as the basis for **interim dividends**.

interim trial balance   Any trial balance prepared at a time before the trial balance which is used as the basis of the preparation of the final accounts.

internal auditor   An employee of an organisation whose job is to examine the effectiveness of the operations within a company, particularly the control systems. Control systems are those used by the management to ensure the correct procedures are used.

internal check   Laying out bookkeeping procedures so that no one clerk enters both the debit and credit entries of any one transaction. This protects the business as well as the clerks, in many cases at no additional cost.

international accounting standard   In order that accounting practice is reasonably consistent throughout the world, the International Accounting Standards Committee has produced and continues to produce suggested standards. There is no law governing the use of such standards but professional accounting bodies would be expected to adhere to them. In the United Kingdom, the Statements of Standard Accounting Practice (SSAPs) have precedence over the International Accounting Standards but they incorporate most of their provisions.

interpretation of final accounts   An explanation of the financial results of a business to make final accounts more easily understood. Thus comparisons can be made with previous years and the performance of a business can be measured by preparing accounting ratios, etc. Interpretation is designed to present the details in a simple way so that a clear picture of the progress and current position of the business can be seen.

inventory   A detailed list of the stocks which are held by a business and their values.

inventory control The procedure that fixes maximum and minimum stock levels. This should ensure that sufficient stock is available to meet the needs of a business but that unnecessary capital is not tied up in surplus stock.

invested capital Same as **capital**.

investment The placing of money in a business, stocks or shares or a bank, in order to obtain a return either in profit, dividends or interest.

invoice A document sent by the seller of goods or services to the customer showing: (a) the goods or services supplied; (b) the cost of the goods/services and the total amount of money due to the seller; (c) other terms relating to the contract. See illustration of **sales invoice** on page 92.

IPFA See **public finance accountant**.

issued capital The amount of share capital that has been issued to shareholders. All of the authorised capital, with which a limited company is registered, need not be issued to shareholders. Directors have the power to decide how much should be issued.

Jj

joint venture A partnership set up to carry out one specific business deal. For example, two builders may agree to jointly renovate a house.

journal (1) The journal is the same as the **journal proper**. See illustration on page 57. (2) A journal is the name which may be given to any book of original entry, e.g. *sales day book* is also known as *sales journal* and *purchases day book*.

journal entry The record of the debit and credit entries to be entered in the ledgers in respect of one transaction, which appears in the **journal proper**. The first accounts entered are the ones to be debited while the second accounts entered are the accounts to be credited.

journal paper Any paper or page ruled with two £ p columns on the right-hand side of the sheet together with date, details and folio column.

journal proper A book of original entry in which the first record is made of the following events: (a) transactions for which no specific book is available. For example, where a simple (unanalysed) purchases day book is used, the credit purchase of an asset is recorded in the journal; (b) transfers between accounts. For example, to allow a provision for depreciation at the year end; (c) correction of errors; (d) opening entries when a business starts. Same as **general journal**.

Journal Layout

Journal of B. Maddison

J18

Date	Details	Folio	dr £ p	cr £ p
May 12	Office Equipment	GL O4	1950·00	
	VAT	GL V1	292·50	
	Goodall's Comp. Shop	PL G3		2242·50
	Credit purchase of computer system – Invoice Nº 615			
July 14	Motor Expenses	GL M2	120·00	
	Motor Car	GL M1		120·00
	Correction of error in posting expenses to asset account.			
July 21	Sales	GL S5	100·00	100·00
	—			
	Correction of overcasting SD Book page 43.			
July 28	Drawings	GL D1	1200·00	
	Rates	GL R2		1200·00
	Transfer of private expenses			

Folio references refer to the account in the ledger to which an entry is posted —

> GL is General ledger
> PL is Purchases ledger
> D1 is Drawings account
> G3 is Goodalls account
> M1 is Motor car account
> M2 is Motor expenses account
> O4 is Office equipment account
> R2 is Rates account
> S5 is Sales account
> V1 is VAT account

Abbreviations: dr=Debit
> cr=Credit

See General ledger account layout (page 47) for posting of July 14 entry.

Kk

Kalamazoo   The name of a limited company that markets stationery and accounting systems. It is well known for its simultaneous entry recording systems which use a pegboard to hold stationery in place. See illustrations of **simultaneous entry** on page 97.

Ll

labour cost   The cost of employing the workforce. See also **direct labour** and **indirect labour.**

last in first out   See **pricing methods.**

lead time   The time taken for delivery of goods after an order has been placed.

lease   A contract by which a lessor gives to a lessee the use of assets for a specified time and payment.

lease types   (a) *finance lease.*   This requires the lessee to repay to the lessor the full cost of the asset together with a return on the investment made by the lessor.   (b) *operating lease*   This requires the lessee to pay rent to hire an asset for a period of time which is usually less than its useful life.

leaseback   An arrangement whereby the buyer of a property leases the property back to the seller.

leasehold   Land or property held by the occupier under a lease.

ledger   (1) A ledger is a book which contains a number of accounts.   (2) The ledger is the main book of accounts which is often for convenience divided into separate books. See also **division of the ledger.**

ledger account   Same as **account.**

lessee   The person (or business) to which an asset is leased.

lessor   The person (or business) which leases an asset.

liability   Something owed by a business; this may be : (a) to its owner; (b) to suppliers of goods/services; (c) to providers of finance.

liability types   (a) *long-term liability*. A liability which is usually repayable more than 12 months after the Balance Sheet date.   (b) *current liability*. A liability which is usually repayable within 12 months of the balance sheet date. Also known as **short term liability**.   (c) *external liability*. Amounts owing to persons or businesses other than shareholders.

LIFO   Abbreviation for **last in first out**. See **pricing methods**.

limited company (Ltd)   A private company which is owned by shareholders whose liability for the debts of the company is limited to the full amount of their shareholding. Regardless of the number of shareholders, the company is treated as a separate legal entity. See also **public limited company.**

limited liability   The principle of law which restricts the shareholders' responsibilities for the debts of the company to their own agreed investment (shareholding) in the company.

limited partnership   A partnership which has at least one partner with limited liability (Limited Partnership Act 1907). These are rare in practice.

liquid assets   Assets which are already, or may be easily turned into cash. Liquid assets consist of debtors, bank and cash.

liquid capital   The surplus or deficit of cash remaining should all the liquid assets be realised to pay the current liabilities. It is calculated as follows:

liquid capital = (current assets−stock)−current liabilities

liquid ratio   A measure which compares liquid assets to current liabilities and shows the result in the form of a ratio. It is calculated as follows:

liquid ratio=current assets−stock : current liabilities.

liquidation   This term is used to describe the process of closing down a company. The legal term for closing down is *winding up*. A company can be wound up compulsorily (See **compulsory winding up)** or voluntarily (See **creditors' voluntary winding up** and **members' voluntary winding up).** In the case of a compulsory winding up, the court will appoint a person to wind up the affairs of the company. This person is called the *Official Receiver*. In the case of a voluntary winding up, the members or creditors will appoint a *liquidator.*

liquidator   A person whose job is to bring the affairs of a company to an end under voluntary winding up. The liquidator will realise the assets, pay the expenses of liquidation and under a creditors' voluntary liquidation, pay the balance of money remaining to the creditors. Under a members' voluntary winding up, the liquidator repays the creditors in full and the balance remaining is returned to shareholders.

liquidity   This is an indicator of the ability of a business to pay its current liabilities by measuring its liquid assets. It may be indicated by various methods. See **liquid capital, liquid ratio** and **acid test ratio.**

list price Same as **catalogue price.**

loan A formal agreement in which a sum of money is borrowed and repaid over a time period.

loan capital Money borrowed for a long period of time which is used to finance permanent expansion of the business e.g. debentures and some bank loans.

lodgement The depositing of monies in a bank account.

long-term liability See **liability types.**

loose leaf ledger A ledger kept in a form in which individual pages may be removed or added.

loss (trading) The condition where costs exceed revenue.

loss types (a) *net loss*. The operating costs exceed the gross profit made on trading and other revenue. (b) *gross loss*. The cost of goods sold exceeds the sales value.

Ltd Abbreviation for **limited company.**

Mm

machine hour method   See **depreciation methods.**

magnetic strip   A strip of magnetic material which is used for electronic storage of information, e.g. name, account number, transaction details. The strip may be used to produce invoices, statements etc. or in bookkeeping.

management accountant   A person who specialises in producing accounting information to help management decision-making.

management accounting   Those accounting procedures concerned with collecting, recording, allocating, analysing and interpreting costs in a way that enables management to understand and control the operations of the business.

management consulting   A service provided by specialists to try to solve problems and improve profitability of organisations.

manufactured goods   Products which are made by a manufacturing process from raw materials or partly made goods.

manufacturing accounts   Accounts prepared to calculate and show the production cost of products completed during the accounting period.

manufacturing cost   Same as **production cost**.

manufacturing profit   The profit deemed to have arisen by manufacturing goods rather than by buying them ready made.

margin   The profit as a percentage of the selling price. See **gross profit margin** and **net profit margin**.

market price   The current price of goods. Depending upon whose viewpoint is taken, it may be either the buying or selling price. As these prices will be different, this term should be used with care.

mark-up   The increase on cost price of goods for sale to allow for seller's profit.

mark-up percentage   The gross profit expressed as a percentage of the buying price. See **gross profit mark-up**.

matching   Fitting like with like.

matching concept   The idea that revenues and expenses shown in a set of accounts should correspond to the accounting period to which the accounts relate. They should not be merely those expenses that have been paid or income received during that period but should include, for example, those expenses unpaid at the end of the period and income due but not received. Same as **accruals concept**.

material requisition note   A document used to request material from stores.

material return note   A document used to record the return of material, for any reason, to stores.

materiality concept   If a financial event significantly affects the profit it should be recorded and shown separately from other events. For example, a small asset may be treated as an expense of the period and charged entirely to the **profit and loss account** (which simplifies business procedures). However, a more expensive asset will be recorded separately. What is material will depend upon the individual business.

maximum stock level   The upper limit beyond which the stock quantity should not be allowed to rise.

mechanised accounting   The use of mechanised powered accounting machines in accounting procedures.

mechanised ledger systems   These use ledger posting machines to make entries on ledger accounts. The machine carries out mechanically procedures previously performed by hand.

media Any material used to store computer data e.g. magnetic tape, floppy disks, hard disk (Winchester disk).

members' equity Same as **shareholders' interest.**

members' voluntary winding up Where a company is able to pay its debts in full, then a members' winding up can take place. Before commencing to wind up, the directors must make a statutory declaration to the effect that the company can pay its debts within a certain period of commencing winding up. Members appoint a *liquidator,* who then proceeds to bring the business to an end and share out whatever money is available to shareholders.

memorandum book A book containing entries which are not a part of the double entry system, e.g. sales day book, daily receipts book.

memorandum column A column in a bookkeeping book containing entries which are not part of the double entry system.

memorandum entry An entry which is made in a memorandum book or column.

memorandum of association One of two documents which govern the actions of a company. This document consists of the following: (a) the name of the company; (b) the location of the registered office in the United Kingdom; (c) the company objectives; (d) details of the authorised share capital; (e) if a **limited company,** a statement that the liability of members (shareholders) is limited; (f) if a **public limited company,** a statement that the company is a public limited company.

menu-driven software A computer program which presents a series of options on the VDU at appropriate stages in the program. The user selects his or her choice of path, through many menus and sub-menus. See illustration on page 65.

minimum stock level The minimum free stock which is always expected to be in stock at any one time.

Menu-Driven Software

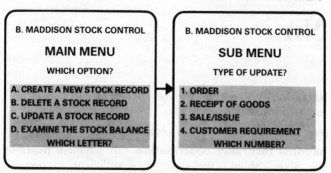

Having chosen option C on Screen 1 the user is presented with
further options on Screen 2.

minority interest The title given to those shareholders who hold less than 50% of the shares in a company.

mispost Same as **error of misposting.**

money A medium of exchange, a store of value, an accounting measuring unit, an investment measuring unit. Its popular form is coins and notes issued by the government.

money measurement concept Accounting measures the transactions of a business only in financial terms. To do this in a consistent and objective way, a standard unit of measure is needed and this is provided by the money used in a country. Money as a unit of measure is frequently confused with money itself. See also **objectivity.**

mortgage A loan which is secured by a transfer of fixed property such as buildings and/or land to the lender *(mortgagee)*. In the event of the loan not being repaid, the lender may seize the property and sell it to obtain repayment of the loan and interest.

mortgagee The person who loans money for a mortgage.

mortgagor The person to whom money is loaned for a mortgage.

Nn

narration   A short explanation of an entry in the journal. See also **journal proper.**

narrative style   Same as **vertical presentation.**

national insurance contribution   A payment made to the State. Should the payer pay sufficient to become eligible, he/she can claim relevant benefit e.g. retirement pension, maternity benefit, unemployment benefit. Employers are required to deduct such contributions from employees wages. There is a minimum wage below which contributions are not payable. It is now effectively an additional income tax.

ncr   Abbreviation for **no carbon required.**

net book value   Same as **written down value (WDV).**

net capital employed   The capital and other finance used by a business as measured by the total value of assets shown on the balance sheet less total liabilities.

net cash flow   The difference between cash receipts and cash payments. A positive or negative cash flow can arise.

net current assets   Same as **working capital.**

net earnings   Earning after deducting all associated costs. See also **net pay.**

net income   Same as **net earnings.**

net loss   See **loss types.**

net pay   The amount of pay received by an employee after all deductions have been made. Same as **net income** and **net earnings.** See also **deductions from pay.**

net present value   The present value of the net cash flow arising over the life of an investment or project. This allows for all future cash receipts and payments discounted to present values, including the initial outlay.

net profit The profit remaining after all expenses have been deducted from gross profit.

net profit margin This is the net profit expressed as a percentage of sales. It is calculated as follows

$$\text{net profit margin} = \frac{\text{net profit} \times 100\%}{\text{sales}}$$

net profit percentage Same as **net profit margin.**

net purchases Purchases less the purchase returns.

net realisable value The amount that would be expected to be received from the sale of stocks after deducting all the expenses that would be incurred in bringing the goods to the point of sale.

net sales Sales less the sales returns. Same as **net turnover**.

net turnover Same as **net sales.**

net working capital Same as **working capital.**

net worth The total value of the business less any external liabilities. The resulting net value represents that belonging to the shareholders or owner(s).

no carbon required (ncr) Stationery that is made specifically to provide copies without the need to use carbon paper.

nominal accounts Those accounts which are concerned with revenue and expenses. For example, sales, purchases, rent (paid and received), discounts etc.

nominal capital Same as **authorised capital.**

nominal ledger The book which contains nominal accounts. See also **general ledger.**

nominal share capital Same as **authorised capital.**

nominal value of a share Shares may be bought and sold at any price, but the nominal value of a share is shown on the share certificate issued to a shareholder and it is registered in the *memorandum of association*. Dividend rates are expressed as a percentage of the nominal value. Also known as *par/face value* of a share.

non-adjusting event   An event which occurs after the balance sheet date and therefore does not change the amounts in the final accounts. However, if a major event has occurred between the balance sheet date and the presentation of the final accounts to shareholders (e.g. a merger, share issues, nationalisation by a government), it is essential that a note be included to this effect in the accounts. This is to ensure that shareholders are kept as informed as possible. To be a major event, it will need to have a significant effect on the financial position of the company. See also **materiality concept.**

non-incorporated business   A business not registered under the Companies Act.

non-profit making organisation   An organisation whose aim is to provide useful services to society or promote an activity. Such a club or institution does not exist for the purpose of trading and/or making a profit. See also **club accounts.**

not negotiable   See **crossed cheques.**

note and coin analysis   Same as **coin and note analysis**. See illustration on page 22.

notice of coding   A form, prepared by the Inland Revenue, notifying an employer of the code number to be applied to the employee's wages for the purpose of income tax deductions. Same as **coding notice.**

Oo

objectivity   The use of general opinion and agreed standards of measurement and a measuring unit (e.g. money) rather than personal opinion, when values or measurements have to be made. In accounting, this means using rules and judgements laid down by accounting bodies. See **concepts of accounting** and **statements of standard accounting practice (SSAP)**.

offsetting accounts   The process of offsetting debit accounts against credit accounts. Where a company is both buying and selling goods from and to the same business, the creditor's account in the purchase ledger may be offset against his or her account in the sales ledger, in which they appear as a debtor. Same as **set-off entries.**

omission error   Same as **error of omission**.

open cheque   A cheque with no crossing which can be used to obtain cash on demand. Cash can be obtained only at the bank branch named on the cheque. See **cheque** and **crossed cheque**.

opening entries   (1) The journal entries which record the position of a business when it first starts trading. The opening entries include any assets (such as motor vehicles, premises, stock, cash) which are contributed to the business by the owner, together with liabilities existing at that date.   (2) The position of a business on the first day of a new financial period.

opening stock   The value of stock at the beginning of a trading period. In an established business, this is the closing stock figure of the previous trading period.

operating costs   This term usually refers to all the costs of a business other than those associated with manufacturing. It includes administrative costs, selling and distribution costs and finance cost.

operating lease   See **lease types**.

operating system   Same as **system software**.

order   An instruction to supply goods or perform work.

order of liquidity   The arrangement of assets into an order in which the most easily cashable (realisable) assets are shown first and those most difficult to convert into cash are shown last. Same as **order of realisability.** See also **liquidity.** Opposite of **order of permanence**.

order of permanence   An arrangement of assets into an order in which the most enduring are shown first and the most liquid item (cash in hand) is shown last. Opposite of **order of liquidity**.

order of realisability   Same as **order of liquidity**.

ordinary share   A fixed and indivisible part of the capital of a company which entitles its owner (a shareholder) to a share of any profit (Note: the holder of preference shares may have preferential rights to any dividends) and/or repayment of capital of liquidation. Same as **equity share.** See also **preference share**.

ordinary shareholders' equity   Same as **ordinary shareholders' interest**.

ordinary shareholders' interest   The total value of the company less external liabilities and preference shareholders' interest. This value is the original capital subscribed plus the profits belonging to the ordinary shareholders, but not distributed to them.

original entry   See **book of original entry.**

outstanding cheques   Cheques paid by a business and not presented to the bank for payment at the date of the bank reconciliation statement.

over-capitalisation   This occurs when a business owns more fixed assets than are appropriate for that type of business. Such over-capitalisation may effect future profitability of the business.

overdraft   A temporary loan made by a bank to a customer who has paid money out of his or her account in excess of the amounts paid in. The prior agreement of the bank manager is usually necessary, as the bank would otherwise not pay a cheque presented for payment if the cheque was for an amount greater than that in the account. See also **bank loan.**

overdraft limit   The limit to which a bank manager will allow cheques to be drawn. The limit represents the maximum overdraft allowed to the account holder.

overhead costs   Any cost which is not a direct cost and cannot therefore be measured directly as a part of the cost of the product is an overhead cost. Overheads are usually analysed into groups such as *production overheads, administration overheads, selling overheads* and *distribution overheads*. An overhead cost can be either a variable cost, a fixed cost or a semi-fixed cost.

oversubscription   If more shares are applied for than are available for issue, then the issue is oversubscribed. Opposite of **undersubscription.**

overtime   When an employee works on a time basis, any extra hours worked above the specified time are overtime. Usually overtime commands a higher rate of pay for the additional time.

overtrading   This occurs where a company's purchases (of both assets and goods for resale) are too high when compared to the capital available. This results in a shortage of working capital as stocks and debtors rise and, more importantly, a reduction in the liquid funds available for paying current bills.

owner's equity   The investment by an owner in his or her business. This investment consists of the original money put into the business plus the profits not withdrawn.

Pp

P45 An employee's leaving certificate which gives details of gross pay and tax deducted up to the date of leaving. Three copies are made by the employer, who sends one to his or her tax office. The employee takes two copies to the new employer, who sends one to his or her (the employer's) tax office and keeps the other. A P45 enables a new employer to deduct tax at the correct rate, and it keeps the Inland Revenue up to date about the employee's whereabouts.

P46 An employee's starting certificate — this form is sent to the Inland Revenue by an employer when a new employee does not have a P45.

P60 A certificate prepared at the end of the tax year by the employer, for each employee, showing gross pay, net pay, income tax deducted, national insurance contributions and other deductions from pay. This is used by the Department of Health and Social Security (DHSS) and the Inland Revenue as a check that payments have been made. The employee's copy is the proof that he or she has paid these amounts.

package (software) Application software which is ready-made for immediate use rather than written to order. A package may contain several programs which are connected in some way. See also **purchases ledger package, sales ledger package, stock package, wages package**.

paid-up capital Sometimes shareholders of a company are asked to pay only a part of the total amount payable on each share. The amount which has actually been paid by all the shareholders is paid-up capital.

par value of a share Same as **nominal value** and **face value of a share**.

partnership A legal term describing a business run by two or more individuals.

Partnership Act 1890 An Act of Parliament passed in 1890 which lays down a set of rules concerning the business affairs of a partnership. The rules are used only where the partners who cannot agree on specific points resort to the law. The main points are :
(a) partners must share equally any profits or losses, and they are entitled to contribute equally to the capital of the business.
(b) no partner has a salary.
(c) no partner has interest on the capital.
(d) if a partner contributes extra capital above his or her share he or she is entitled to 5% interest per year.
(e) the books of the business must be kept at the ordinary place of business and must be available for any partner to see and copy.
(f) no new partner may be brought into the business without general consent.

partnership agreement An agreement between partners about the running of their partnership. This may be: (a) an oral agreement (proved by witnesses); (b) an agreement implied by the actions of partners, e.g. accepting divisions of profits; (c) an informal written agreement; (d) a formal partnership deed. See also **partnership deed.**

partnership appropriation The distribution of profits (or losses) to the partners in a partnership. See also **appropriation account.**

partnership capital The total capital invested in a partnership. Each partner has a separate capital account which shows the amount of capital he has contributed.

partnership deed A formal agreement of partners. Such an agreement would usually cover at least the following points :

(a)   the amount of capital contributed by each partner.
(b)   the rate of interest (if any) on the capital.
(c)   whether salaries are to be paid to any partners.
(d)   how profits or losses are to be shared among the partners.
(e)   the limit on drawings for each partner, and any interest paid on drawings.
(f)   procedures on the death of a partner or on how the partnership may be dissolved.

Same as **deed of partnership.** See also **partnership agreement.**

partnership drawings   The drawings taken from a partnership by partners. These are recorded in separate drawings accounts for each partner. Interest may be charged on drawings if agreed.

partnership final accounts   These consist of a **balance sheet, profit and loss account** and an **appropriation account.**

partnership salary   Where a partner works wholly or part-time in running the partnership business, it is usual to pay him or her a salary out of the profits.

patent rights   A patent gives the sole right to manufacture and sell a product. It is an intangible asset. As such it is shown as a fixed asset on the balance sheet, often with only a nominal value (£1). Patent rights have no 'true' value other than any amounts paid to purchase them. They are shown to prove the company has these rights. See also **trademarks** and **copyright**.

pay   Money given for service. See also **salary** and **wages.**

pay advice   Same as payslip.

pay as you earn (PAYE)   A system operated by an employer on behalf of the Inland Revenue to collect income tax from employees when they are paid. The tax is deducted from gross pay and only the net earnings are given to the employee.

payback   A term used in determining the length of time taken for an investment to earn, recover or pay back the original sum invested.

PAYE   Same as **Pay As You Earn.**

payee   A person to whom money is paid.

paying-in book   A book of paying-in slips and counterfoils which is given to bank customers who regularly pay notes, coins and cheques into the bank. The customer completes the paying-in slip and counterfoil giving details of payment. This is checked by the bank and the counterfoil is stamped as a receipt.

payments in advance   An expense which has been paid before the end of the period to which it relates, the benefit of which may extend into the following accounting period. Some payments are always made in advance, e.g. insurance premiums, where the first premium must be paid before the insurance is effective.

payroll   (1) A list of employees and the payments to which they are entitled.   (2) The calculation of the amounts payable to employees.

payroll sheet   A record which is kept by a business and shows the details of every employee's pay and deductions.

Payslip or Pay Advice

PAY ADVICE	Details — This Week/Month		NAME T. BLACK	
TOTALS TO DATE	BASIC	180·00	MONTH/WEEK ENDING 300586	
TOTAL GROSS 1650·50	OVERTIME	12·50	TAX CODE 355	
TAXABLE NET 1650·50	ALLOWANCES	–	N.I. NUMBER ST000102	
TAX 313·60	GROSS PAY	192·50	N.I. CATEGORY A	
SUPER-ANNUATION –	DEDUCTIONS — TAX	35·55	METHOD OF PAY CASH	
N.I. 123·78	N.I.	14·45	BANK CODE –	
NOTES:	SUPERANNUATION	–	ACCOUNT No. –	
	OTHERS	–		
	TOTAL	50·00	EMPLOYEE	
	NET PAY	142·50	PAY REFERENCE 001	

payslip   A notification given to an employee which shows details of his wages or salary. Often a salary is paid directly into the employee's bank account but a payslip is still given to the employee. See illustration on page 75.

pegboard   A board which allows several documents to be aligned and held, enabling an entry to be made simultaneously on the documents by the use of ncr or carbon paper. See also **simultaneous accounting records** illustration on page 97.

pension contributions   See **national insurance contribution** and **superannuation contributions.**

personal account   The account of a person, firm or company. Usually refers to a debtor's or creditor's account. For other types of account see **account classes.**

personal ledger   A ledger which contains personal accounts. Usually refers to the **sales ledger** and the **purchase ledger.**

petty cash   Miscellaneous small sums of money which are received or paid out.

petty cash book   A subsidiary to the cash book which records petty cash transactions such as purchases of small items of stationery and reimbursement of travelling expenses. Most petty cash books are analysed and work on the Imprest system, which simplifies procedures for the petty cashier.

petty cash voucher   A voucher which gives details of a petty cash expense, to which is attached any relevant receipts. It usually requires signature by an authorised person. Some businesses use vouchers as proof of an expense, which the petty cashier must be given before payment is made. See illustration on page 77.

petty cashier   The person who keeps the petty cash book.

piecework   A system where each employee is paid according to the number of goods he or she has produced or processed. A rate of pay is fixed per 'piece' or quantity of goods produced.

Petty Cash Voucher

PETTY CASH VOUCHER		No. 102
Details of Expenses	£	p
Petrol for Motor Van	£15·00	

PAID TO: *T. Black*   RECEIVED: *T. Black*   DATE: *2/6*
RECEIPTS ATTACHED: *Yes*
AUTHORISED: *Brian Maddison*

piecework system   Where employees are paid by piece-work, the system normally provides for a minimum wage, based on an hourly rate, to be paid when piecework earnings are below this figure.

PLC/plc   Abbreviations for **public limited company.**

post dated cheque   A cheque made out with a date in the future.

postal order   A convenient method of sending small sums of money through the post. Orders are purchased at post offices. The maximum value is at present £20. Postal orders have fixed values and a *poundage charge* (or fee) is made according to the value. The sender of a postal order enters the payee's name and can specify the post office of payment. A crossed postal order can only be paid through a bank.

posting   The operation of transferring entries or totals of entries from a book to an account in a ledger. The totals in day books must be posted to the relevant ledger accounts. Also some entries may need to be posted from one ledger account to another.

preference share   A share (part ownership) in a company which may entitle its owner (a preference shareholder) to a specified rate of dividend from the profit. Any remaining profit is then used to pay dividends to ordinary shareholders. Also, in the event of the company winding up, preference shareholders may be preferential to ordinary shareholders in the repayment of their capital. Preference shares may be *cumulative* or *non-cumulative*. Cumulative preference shares entitle the holder to arrears of dividends unpaid in previous years, before any profits are available to ordinary shareholders.

preliminary expenses   The expenses incurred when a company is being formed, i.e. prior to its incorporation as a limited company. Examples are legal expenses and stamp duties. Same as **formation expenses.**

premiums on debentures   A premium is an amount, over and above the nominal value, repaid by the borrower to the debenture holder on the repayment of a loan.

premiums on preference shares   (1) An amount, above the nominal value, paid by the shareholder upon subscribing for his shareholding.   (2) An amount, over and above the nominal value, repaid by the company when redeeming redeemable preference shares.

prepaid charges or expenses   Same as **payments in advance.**

prepayments   Same as **payments in advance.**

present day value   This represents: (a) the replacement price of an existing asset; (b) the realisable value if an existing asset is sold; (c) the cost of buying a service now or the income to be received from supplying a service now.

present value   This is a term used in the procedures for calculating how much cash received in the future is worth now. It is the value now of a sum to be received in the future. For example, if the interest rates are 10% per annum, then £1000 to be received in one year's time has the present value of £909.09. The future sum of £1000 is described as being discounted to the present value.

price   The amount for which an item is sold or offered for sale. Usually an amount of money.

price-earning ratio The ratio of the share price of a company, as shown by the stock market, to the earnings per share.

pricing methods These are methods of putting a value on material issued from stock. A method having been chosen, it should be used consistently. Pricing methods are:

(a) *first in first out* (FIFO): materials are used at the price of the earliest materials received which are still in stock.

(b) *last in first out* (LIFO): materials are issued at the price of the latest materials received which are still in stock.

(c) *weighted average*: materials are issued at the average cost of the stocks held at the time of issue. A new average cost is normally calculated immediately on receipt of goods or materials. Same as **average cost (AVCO)**.

primary efficiency ratio Same as **return on capital.**

prime cost The basic cost of manufacturing a product, i.e. the total cost of direct materials, direct labour and direct expense. No overheads are included.

prime entry, book of Same as **book of original entry.**

principal The name given to any person who has given authority to an agent to act on their behalf.

private expenses Same as **drawings.**

private ledger A part of the nominal ledger, used when the owner of a business wishes to keep some accounts as private. The accounts in the private ledger usually include the capital account, drawings account and trading, profit and loss acount. The owner may also which to keep other accounts private (e.g. loan accounts).

private limited company See **limited company.**

production budget See **budget.**

production cost The cost of manufacturing a product, i.e. the prime cost and the overhead costs involved in production. Same as **factory cost, work cost** and **manufacturing cost.**

production overheads The cost of operating the factory, production line or process, *other* than the direct costs (direct labour, direct materials and direct expenses). These will include the wages of supervisors, storemen, labourers, maintenance men and also heating, lighting, insurance and all other costs.

profit An increase in the net assets of a business. This can arise from revenue profits or capital profits. In real terms it is the difference between what is destroyed (materials and labour) in the production of 'a good' or service and the value of the good or service produced. Primarily a subjective judgement, it is translated into an objective one by accountants using the money measurement concept.

profit and loss account An account which shows the profit or loss made by a business during a period of trading. The profit and loss account is a ledger account which forms part of the final accounts. It shows expenses to be deducted from the gross profit and other sources of income to be added to gross profit. See also **revenue account.**

profit appropriation See **appropriation account.**

profit budget The planned profit to be achieved by the budgeted activities. See also **budget.**

profit margin See **gross profit margin** and **net profit margin.**

provision An amount set aside out of profits so as to be prepared for a future anticipated loss, the extent of which is not yet known. Provisions would be made for bad debts, depreciation, discounts and for replacement of assets.

prudence concept The rule which requires a careful or prudent view to be taken in calculating the profit of a business. If there is any possibility of a loss arising from the current activities, a provision should be made to cover the anticipated loss. However, anticipated profits are not brought into account. Same as **conservatism concept.**

public finance accountant   A member of the Chartered Institute of Public Finance and Accountancy **(IPFA).**

public limited company   A company registered with a memorandum which states that the company is to be a public limited company. The allotted share capital must not be less than the minimum specified by law, at present £50 000.   The company must use the term *public limited company* at the end of its name, or the abbreviations *PLC* or *plc.*

published accounts   See **company accounts.**

purchase   Anything bought.

purchase invoice   See **invoice.**

purchase order   An official business document, ordering the supply of goods or services, sent to the supplier by the purchaser.

purchase requisition   A document sent to the purchase department, or buyer, in a business. A purchase requisition is sent by a person who is authorised to do so, ordering goods or services.

purchase return   Goods bought by a business which are returned to the supplier because they are unsatisfactory or unsuitable.

purchase book   Same as **purchases day book.**

purchases day book   The book of original entry which records all the credit purchases of goods and services. See illustration on page 82.

purchases journal   Same as **purchases day book.**

purchases ledger   A book containing the accounts of creditors. Each credit purchase is credited to the account of the appropriate creditor. See illustration on page 83.

Purchases daybook layout

Purchases Day Book of B. Maddison   PDB9

			PL	INVOICE TOTAL		NET PURCHASES		VAT	
May	1	A. Creddor Ltd.	C1	66	70	58	00	8	70
"	6	R. Jones & Son	J2	1025	80	892	00	133	80
"	8	A. Wooler	W1	2542	65	2211	00	331	65
"	18	A. Creddor Ltd.	C1	84	06	73	10	10	96
"	20	W. Argus	A2	18	40	16	00	2	40
"	20	V. Smith	S4	102	35	89	00	13	35
"	25	A. Creddor Ltd.	C1	55	20	48	00	7	20
"	27	A. Wooler	W1	3061	30	2662	00	399	30
"	27	A. Creddor Ltd.	C1	120	32	104	63	15	69
"	28	R. Jones & Son	J2	1026	95	893	00	133	95
"	30	Fish Bros.	F2	64	40	56	00	8	40
				8168	13	7102	73	1065	40
				GL C2		GL P1		GL V1	
June	1	T. Cornwallis & Co.	C3	57	50	50	00	7	50
"	1	Woodward (Supplies) Ltd.	W2	92	00	80	00	12	00
"	2	W. Argus	A2	10	35	9	00	1	35
"	3	A. Creddor	C1	75	90	66	00	9	90

Individual purchases are posted to their creditor's account.
Total of invoices is posted to Purchases ledger control account.
Total of net purchases is posted to Purchases account.
Total of VAT is posted to VAT account.
See also Purchases ledger account layout (page 83).

purchases ledger control account   The account summarising the ledger accounts of creditors. See also **control
account.**

purchases ledger package   A set of computer programs
which will keep a purchases ledger. This mainly involves
maintaining suppliers' accounts. Other features are often
included, e.g. (a) a purchases day book is kept; (b) cheques
are printed ready for payment; (c) ageing schedules of
creditors are produced; (d) various analyses of purchases
may be made.

Purchases Ledger Account Layout
Purchases Ledger of B. Maddison

A. Greddor Ltd.   Account C1

Date	Details	Folio	£ p	Date	Details	Folio	£ p
		b/f		19-9		b/f	92·63
May1	Bank	CB 26	92·63	May1	Purchases	PDB 9	66·70
23	Bank	26	66·70	" 18	— " —	9	84·06
				" 25	— " —	9	55·20
31	Balance	c/d	259·58	" 27	— " —	9	120·32
			418·91				418·91
				June 1	Balance	b/d	259·58
				" 3	Purchases	PDB 9	75·90
		c/f				c/f	

Folio references refer to the page number in the book of original entry from which this entry is posted — PDB is Purchases day book, CB is cash book.

Abbreviations: b/f=Brought forward
c/d=Carried down
c/f=Carried forward
See Purchases day book layout (page 82) for source of May entries.

purchases returns book A book of original entry which records the returns of goods bought on credit. Same as **returns outwards book.**

purchases returns day book Same as **purchases returns book.**

pyramid of ratios A set of ratios subsidiary to the return on capital which are used to measure the performance of a business. See illustration on page 84.

Pyramid of Ratios

Pyramid of Ratios

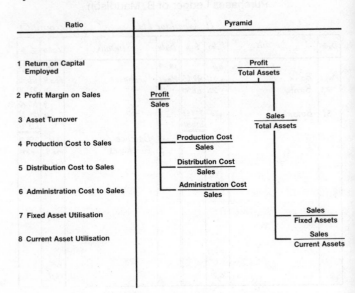

Ratio	Pyramid

1. Return on Capital Employed

2. Profit Margin on Sales

3. Asset Turnover

4. Production Cost to Sales

5. Distribution Cost to Sales

6. Administration Cost to Sales

7. Fixed Asset Utilisation

8. Current Asset Utilisation

$$\frac{\text{Profit}}{\text{Total Assets}}$$

$$\frac{\text{Profit}}{\text{Sales}}$$

$$\frac{\text{Sales}}{\text{Total Assets}}$$

$$\frac{\text{Production Cost}}{\text{Sales}}$$

$$\frac{\text{Distribution Cost}}{\text{Sales}}$$

$$\frac{\text{Administration Cost}}{\text{Sales}}$$

$$\frac{\text{Sales}}{\text{Fixed Assets}}$$

$$\frac{\text{Sales}}{\text{Current Assets}}$$

Note: Profit Margin on Sales × Asset Turnover = Return on Capital Employed

$$\frac{\text{Profit}}{\text{Sales}} \times \frac{\text{Sales}}{\text{Total Assets}} = \frac{\text{Profit}}{\text{Total Assets}}$$

Qq

quantity discount   See **discount types**.

quick ratio   Same as **liquid ratio**.

quoted investment   Investments made by an investor (an individual or a company) which are traded on the Stock Exchange and therefore have a value quoted on the Stock Exchange.

Rr

rate of return   The measure of the income received by an investor from an investment. It is calculated by measuring the income as a percentage of the amount invested.

rate of stock turnover   The number of times the average stock has been sold and replaced with new stock during a year. It is calculated as follows:

$$\text{rate of stock turnover} = \frac{\text{cost of goods sold}}{\text{average stock held (at cost price)}}$$

rates   An amount charged by a local authority to a ratepayer. The amount is assessed on the value of the ratepayer's property.

ratio   A relationship between one quantity and another.

ratio analysis   A method in which accounting data is expressed as a proportion of other data and which measures the performance of a business.

ratio types   Ratios can be calculated between almost any accounting data. Listed below are some commonly quoted accounting ratios (many of which are not expressed as a ratio, but as a single number):

   asset turnover ratio
   liquid ratio
   mark-up ratio
   profit margin
   rate of stock turnover
   return on capital

See separate entries.

raw materials   (1) Materials which are in their natural condition and have not been changed by manufacture or processing.   (2) The materials used by a firm or industry. For example, the raw materials of ship-building are sheet steel, steel bars etc., which are the finished products of the steel-making companies. See also **direct material.**

R/D   Abbreviation for **refer to drawer.** See **dishonour.**

real account   An account which records transactions relating to a tangible asset so that the value of the asset can be seen. This value is normally the cost price.

real asset   Same as **tangible asset.**

realisation concept   For bookkeeping and accounting purposes it is important to know when a financial event has taken place. The realisation concept gives *acceptance* of goods or services as a basis for deciding whether goods have been bought or sold. For example, when goods are bought on credit, once the invoice is received it is considered that the goods have been accepted. Similarly goods sold on credit are considered accepted as soon as the invoice is issued. It is not necessary to wait for payment or receipt of the goods.

realisability   The ease with which an asset can be converted into cash.

receipt   (1) Money received by a business.   (2) A document which serves as evidence of payment.

receipts and payments account   An account used by non-profit-making organisations giving a summary of all the receipts and payments recorded in the cash book.

receiver   An officer appointed by the court to deal with the winding up of a company under a compulsory winding up order, or to take over the affairs of a company and operate the company in the interest of debenture holders.

recognised accounting bodies
(a)   The Institute of Chartered Accountants in England and Wales.
(b)   The Institute of Chartered Accountants of Scotland.
(c)   The Institute of Chartered Accountants in Ireland.
(d)   The Institute of Cost and Management Accountants.
(e)   The Chartered Association of Certified Accountants.
(f)   The Chartered Institute of Public Finance and Accountancy.

reconciliation statement   A statement which enables reconciliation of events with another record of the same events, where differences have arisen because of time separation of events, e.g. the time required to despatch and deliver goods, a cheque lost in the post. See also **bank reconciliation statement.**

reducing balance method   See **depreciation methods.**

refer to drawer   See **dishonour.**

reference   A statement giving information relating to a person or organisation. It usually details qualities, experience and qualifications and, occasionally, financial status.

registered capital   Same as **authorised capital.**

registered office See **memorandum of association.**

remittance Money which has been sent, usually by post.

remittance advice A statement accompying a remittance from a debtor saying which item or items the remittance is paying. If there is no remittance advice, the creditor may allocate the remittance. A detachable form is sometimes attached to an invoice for the convenience of the debtor.

reserve Profit which has been set aside for general purposes and thereby retained in the business.

reserve types (a) *Capital reserves* are those which are of a capital nature. For example, as a result of share or debenture premiums and revaluation of assets, these may be distributed to shareholders as bonus shares, but not in cash. (b) *Revenue reserves* are sums which have been set aside out of profits for various purposes. Examples are for replacement of assets or, in a general reserve, so that unexpected losses can be met or the business expanded without raising further capital.

residual value The expected selling price of an asset at the end of its useful life.

return on capital The measure which compares the net profit (as shown in the profit and loss account) with the owner's capital. This is an important measure since it shows the owner's return on investment. It is calculated as follows:

$$\text{return on capital} = \frac{\text{net profit} \times 100\%}{\text{total assets} - \text{long term liabilities}}$$

Same as **primary efficiency ratio** and **return on capital employed.**

return on capital employed Same as **return on capital.**

return on equity ratio   A measure which shows the return earned on the ordinary shareholders' interest.

returns   (1) Goods which have been returned to the supplier because they are unsatisfactory or unsuitable. (2) Returnable containers which are returned for refund.

returns inwards   Same as **sales returns.**

returns outwards   Same as **purchase returns.**

returns to store   Materials previously issued for use, which have now been returned to the store.

revaluation depreciation method   See **depreciation methods.**

revaluation of assets   Asset values vary with time. Whilst most assets decrease in value, some assets (such as land and buildings) may increase in value. Revaluation of these assets is important to ensure that assets are not undervalued. See also **depreciation methods:** *revaluation depreciation.*

revenue   (1) The return or income obtained from an investment.   (2) The income received by government from taxes and licences.

revenue account   (1) The name for the profit and loss account of a business which is selling services. Used for example by professional business partnerships such as lawyers and dentists since no trading is taking place.   (2) A general term to include the manufacturing, trading and profit and loss and appropriate accounts. See illustration on page 90.

revenue expenditure   Money used to pay for revenue expenses.

revenue expenses   The expenses resulting from the day

Revenue Account Layout

```
                        B. MADDISON

               T/A B. MADDISON (GLAZIERS)

          Revenue Account for the Year Ended 31st July 1987


                                          £        £

Sales                                             21243

Less Expenses:
   Advertising                           123
   Accountancy Fees                      360
   Sub Contractors                      1560
   Motor Expenses                       2220
   Miscellaneous Expenses                 91
   Telephones                             94
   Bank Charges & Interest              140
   Materials                            8696
   Insurance                             98
   Use of Home as Office                 52
   Protective Clothes & Laundry         118
   Printing, Postage & Stationery        17
   Interest on Loan                     160
   Depreciation:
      Van                               572
      Car (1)                           645
      Car (2)                           237
      Tools                              -
      Office Equipment                    4      15187

                                                  6056

   Add: Interest Received                35
   Less: Loss on Van Disposal            20        15

   Net Profit for the Year                       £6071
```

to day running of a business. This includes goods for resale, consumable items and services.

revenue income   Income arising from the daily sales of goods and/or services by a business.

revenue profit   The profit made on the normal daily trading or service activities of the business.

90

revenue receipts   Money received as a result of the normal trading or service activities of a business.

revenue reserve   See **reserve types**.

reversal of figures error   See **error of transposition**.

running balance   Same as **continuous balance**.

Ss

salary   The name given to wages paid to office workers. Payment is usually made monthly although the salary is often quoted as an annual figure.

sale of assets   See **disposal of assets**.

sales   The value of goods or services which have been sold by a business. Same as **turnover**.

sales analysis book   See **analysed book**.

sales book   Same as **sales day book**.

Sales Invoice

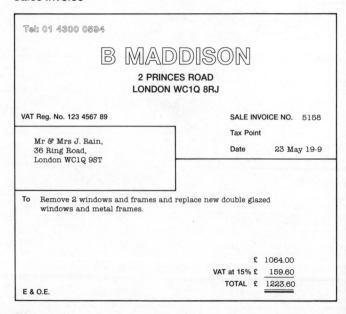

Tel: 01 4300 0594

B MADDISON
2 PRINCES ROAD
LONDON WC1Q 8RJ

VAT Reg. No. 123 4567 89

SALE INVOICE NO.   5158

Tax Point

Mr & Mrs J. Rain,
36 Ring Road,
London WC1Q 9ST

Date   23 May 19-9

To   Remove 2 windows and frames and replace new double glazed windows and metal frames.

	£	1064.00
VAT at 15%	£	159.60
TOTAL	£	1223.60

E & O.E.

sales budget   See **budget**.

sales day book   The book of original entry which records all the credit sales of goods and services.

sales invoice   A document prepared by the seller for a customer who is buying goods or services on credit. The invoice gives details of both the buyer and seller, goods purchased and their price, and the trading terms applicable. See illustration on page 92.

sales journal   Same as **sales day book**.

sales ledger   A book containing the accounts of debtors. Each credit sale is recorded in the account of the appropriate debtor.

sales ledger control account   The account summarising the ledger accounts of debtors. See also **control account**.

sales ledger package   A set of computer programs which will keep a sales ledger. This mainly involves maintaining customers accounts. Other features are often included, e.g. (a) a sales day book is kept; (b) ageing schedules of debtors are produced; (c) the amount of VAT charged is recorded; (d) monthly statements are printed to send to customers.

sales returns   Goods sold by a business which are returned by the customer because they are unsatisfactory or unsuitable. Same as **returns inwards**.

sales returns book   A book of original entry which records the returns of goods which were sold on credit. Same as **returns inwards book**.

sales returns day book   Same as **sales returns book**.

sales to fixed assets ratio   This is the ratio of sales (turnover) to fixed assets. The ratio is usually expressed as a number which is calculated as follows:

$$\text{sales to fixed assets ratio} = \frac{\text{sales}}{\text{fixed assets}}$$

This ratio is a measure of how effectively the business is using its total assets to generate sales. Same as **fixed asset utilisation ratio**.

schedule of debtors   Same as **ageing schedule**.

sectional balancing   Where control accounts are used, it is often the practice to prepare total figures for one group of debtors, e.g. those beginning with letters A-D. By dividing the ledger in this way, each section of the books is balanced separately.

secured debentures   A loan made to a company which gives the debenture holder the right to take over a specific asset (or group of assets) if loan repayments or interest payments are not made. See also **floating debenture**.

securities   The Stock Exchange term for stocks and shares.

self-balancing ledgers   This term applies where an adjustment account is used to summarise ledger entries. This means there is a continuous check on the double entry system, because the adjustment account is the same as a control account with all the entries reversed.

selling costs   The costs of employing sales staff, buying advertising and promoting products.

selling price   The price at which goods are sold to customers after deduction of any trade discount.

semi-fixed costs   Costs such as telephone expenses, which have two elements. One element is a *fixed* cost (rental charges) and the other is *variable* (the cost according to the length and type of call).

service business accounts   A business which provides a service needs to prepare a revenue account. This account compares the income received from providing the services with the costs incurred, and shows the net profit or loss. As the business is not selling goods, a trading account is not required.

services rendered   Services provided by a business to a customer are usually referred to on the invoice to the customer as 'services rendered'.

set-off entries   Same as **offsetting accounts**.

Share Certificate

SHARE CERTIFICATE

N°

LIMITED

This is to Certify that

of

is the Registered Proprietor of

Fully Paid   Shares of

each, numbered   to   inclusive in the above-named Company subject to the Memorandum and Articles of Association thereof

Given under the Common Seal of the Company the   day of   19

SECRETARY.

DIRECTORS.

share capital The money that a company has obtained or could obtain from shareholders, who receive share certificates as evidence of their investment. See also **issued capital** and **authorised capital**.

share capital account The account recording the capital issued to shareholders.

share certificate A document issued by a company under seal to a shareholder showing ownership of one or more shares in the company. See illustration above.

share premium Any amount over the nominal value of a share that a company can ask prospective shareholders to pay. If shares are likely to be in great demand then a large premium can be charged.

shareholders Persons who own shares in a company and are therefore part owners of a company. A shareholder can be an individual or a company.

95

shareholders' equity   Same as **shareholders' interest**.

shareholders' funds   Same as **shareholders' interest**.

shareholders' interest   The investment made by shareholders in a company. This investment will be represented by the original capital subscribed by the shareholders plus the profits belonging to the shareholders, but not distributed to them.

shares   The name given to the capital that a company has raised from people who wish to own a part of that company.

short term liability   See **liability types:** *current liabilities*.

short term loan   A loan that will require to be repaid within a short time — usually within a year.

simultaneous accounting records   A system in which two or more accounting records can be entered (recorded) at the same time. This is achieved using stationery (with *ncr* or carbon paper) which is located and held in position so that one written entry appears on several records. See illustration on page 97.

simultaneous entry   An entry made on a record which simultaneously appears on one or two other records. See **simultaneous accounting records**.

single entry   A simple bookkeeping system in which the records show only one aspect of each transaction (under the double entry principle, both aspects of a transaction are recorded). Often a cash book is the only record kept, which shows receipts and payments. This system is usually used by sole traders because of its simplicity — although preparation of the final accounts, by an accountant, is more time-consuming and therefore costly.

sinking fund account   This fund may be the same as a provision for depreciation but is also used to build up funds to pay long term liabilities, e.g. debentures. Its use indicates that cash is being set aside for the asset replacement. The cash invested is recorded in a sinking fund investment account.

Simultaneous Accounting Records
Sales Ledger Example

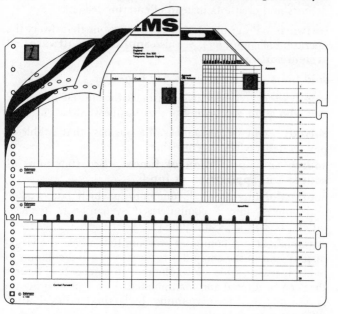

1 Sales day book sheet positioned firstly on the pegboard (collator).

2 Sales ledger card placed on pegboard and aligned. (First vacant line on the ledger card is placed over the first vacant line on the journal).

3 Statement aligned on to the ledger card.

sinking fund investment account The account recording the money invested by a business to replace an asset when the asset's life expires or to discharge a long term liability.

slip system A bookkeeping system in which invoices received and copy sales invoices replace the books of original entry. The documents themselves are filed or

97

bound together to form a book of original entry. Copies of these invoices are used to maintain personal accounts of debtors and creditors instead of entering ledgers.

software   Programs or sets of instructions that direct the operation of computers. See also **application software** and **system software**.

sold book   Same as **sales day book**.

sole trader   A person in business by himself or herself and who is the sole owner of that business.

solvent   The circumstances of a business that is able to pay its debts when they are due.

source and application of funds   See **statement of source and application of funds**.

source document   A document from which data is taken and entered into a computerised system, e.g. invoices, orders, receipt slips and time cards.

spreadsheet   A computer program that allows the visual display unit of the computer to act as rows and columns of analysis paper. This allows the user to enter sets of figures that can be altered and manipulated. This type of program is typically used for accounting, budgeting and evaluating different financial policies.

SSAP   Abbreviation for **statement of standard accounting practice**.

> **SSAP 1**:   accounting for associated companies.
> **SSAP 2**:   disclosure of accounting policies.
> **SSAP 3**:   earnings per share.
> **SSAP 4**:   the accounting treatment of government grants.
> **SSAP 5**:   accounting for value added tax.
> **SSAP 6**:   extraordinary items and prior year adjustments.
>   SSAP 7 withdrawn.
> **SSAP 8**:   the treatment of taxation under the imputation system in the accounts of companies.

SSAP 9: stocks and work in progress.

SSAP 10: statements of source and application of funds.

SSAP 11 withdrawn.

SSAP 12: accounting for depreciation.

SSAP 13: accounting for research and development.

SSAP 14: group accounts.

SSAP 15: accounting for deferred taxation.

SSAP 16 withdrawn.

SSAP 17: accounting for post-balance sheet events.

SSAP 18: accounting for contingencies.

SSAP 19: accounting for investment properties.

SSAP 20: foreign currency translation.

SSAP 21: accounting for leases and hire purchase contracts.

SSAP 22: accounting for goodwill.

SSAP 23: accounting for acquisitions and mergers.

standard costs   The planned costs which a business expects to incur. Unless a measure of what is expected exists, it is impossible to compare the actual costs in a way that enables control to be effective. Examples of such costs are the expected cost of making one item of the product, the budgeted costs of operating a department, the expected cost of carrying out one operation in the factory.

standard rate (VAT)   The rate of VAT added to taxable goods or services supplied, other than zero-rated supplies and exempt supplies. Registered traders should be no better or worse off because of VAT. They collect and pay to Customs and Excise the VAT paid to them, and reclaim any VAT paid by them. Only the final customer actually pays VAT. It is effectively a heavy turnover tax on those services which cannot add on the impost, e.g. hairdressing, floristry etc. (Note: impost=tax).

standing order   An instruction to the bank to make regular payments on behalf of an account holder. For example, monthly rates or rents, hire purchase payments. Using a standing order, the account holder is saved the work of writing out cheques at regular intervals.

statement (of account)   The term statement usually refers to a statement of account. This is a copy of the account of a customer (in the books of the supplier) that is sent monthly to the customer. The statement enables the customer to reconcile the supplier's account with his or her own record and acts as a reminder to the customers of the amounts due. Banks (which may be debtors or creditors) send regular statements to their account holders.

statement of affairs   (1) A statement in the form of a balance sheet drawn up when it is not possible to prepare final accounts and a balance sheet owing to incomplete books and accounts. The statement of affairs will show the estimated amounts of assets and external liabilities, the difference being the owner's capital at that date.   (2) The statement drawn up to show a debtor's position in bankruptcy or liquidation and the expected realisable values of assets and total of creditors.

statement of recommended practice (SORP)   A recommended method of dealing in the accounts with a particular accounting matter. These recommendations are developed and issued by the Accounting Standards Committee on subjects which do not require a **statement of standard accounting practice**.

statement of source and application of funds   A statement summarising the sources of funds received and the uses made of those funds. Detailed in **SSAP 10.**

statements of standard accounting practice (SSAP)
Methods and procedures for dealing with accounting matters. These procedures are mandatory on all members of the professional accountancy bodies. The statements are prepared by the Accounting Standards Committee which is

representative of the six chartered accounting bodies in the UK. The titles of SSAP 1 to SSAP 23 are shown under **SSAP**.

statutory deductions   Amounts required by the State to be taken off the wages of employees by employers. Income tax and national insurance contributions are the two main deductions.

stock account   In a small business, this account will show only the opening and closing stock valuations of each year. A larger business may maintain a stock ledger. This records the value of both receipts and issues, and the stock account will show the value of stock held by the business at any time. Stock categories are:

(a) *components* — ready-made parts purchased for inclusion in the product being made.

(b) *consumable materials*, e.g. spare parts, oils, towels.

(c) *finished goods* — manufactured products ready for sale.

(d) *goods for resale* — goods purchased in a saleable condition which may be resold.

(e) *raw materials* — materials which will be altered by processing or manufacture into the final product of that business.

(f) *work in progress* — semi-manufactured parts, semi-processed materials or partly completed products.

stock control card   A record of stock movements in stores. Stock control cards record: (a) the quantity of stock in and out; (b) the materials required for factory jobs; (c) the materials ordered; (d) the materials not delivered; (e) the materials available to meet new requirements.

stock ledger   The ledger which contains stock accounts. An account is kept for each item of stock which usually shows: (a) the quantities received; (b) the cost of the quantities received; (c) the quantities issued; (d) the price of each issue; (e) the stock balance; (f) the value of the stock balances.

stock package   A set of computer programs which will keep an inventory of all stock. This involves keeping records of each stock item, such as description, price, minimum and maximum quantities to be stocked and stock movements. Other features are often included, e.g. (a) supplier's names and addresses; (b) immediate enquiry facilities to show current stock values; (c) forecasts of stock requirements based on previous figures; (d) value of stock on hand.

stock pricing   The valuing of materials issued to a factory and goods issued or sold by a trading business. Stock pricing is essential to calculate the cost of a manufactured product. Also profits in a trading business are calculated by comparing sales income with cost price. See also **pricing methods**.

stock record   The general term which describes a document showing the receipts and issues of stock into and out of the stores. Other details will be kept on the record, depending upon its use. For example, a bin card may require location details. See also **bin card**, **stock control card** and **stock ledger**.

stock take   A physical check of stock, usually at the year end, to verify the quantities of stock that exist and their condition. The value of stock included in the final accounts is based on the quantity of stock held and therefore a proper stock take is essential.

stock turnover   The rate at which stock is sold and replaced. It is calculated as follows:

$$\text{stock turnover per year} = \frac{\text{cost of goods sold in the year}}{\text{average stock held during the year (at cost price)}}$$

stock valuation   A money valuation of the stocks held. Whenever a set of final accounts is prepared, the value of stocks on hand needs to be determined. If a continuous inventory is not operated then the business will need a stock take. The different stock categories will need to be valued individually at the lower of cost price or the net realisable value.

stocks   (1) The value or quantity of materials held by a business. See also **stock categories.**   (2) The name of an investment made by a person or business which takes the form of a loan to either the government, public authority or a limited company. Such stocks are also called *bonds, debentures* or *loans* and they are traded on the Stock Exchange.

stores requisitions   A document used to request materials from stores. Same as **material requisition note.**

straight line method   See **depreciation methods.**

style of final account   See **horizontal presentation** and **vertical presentation.**

subjectivity   A personal view or opinion of a matter, coloured by personal feelings and ignoring the views or opinions of others. In order to overcome the variety of subjective views of accountants, all dealing with the same or similar matters, the accountancy bodies developed the **statements of standard accounting practices**. These standards are designed to bring objectivity to the treatment of accountancy matters.

subscribed capital   The amount of issued capital that shareholders have agreed to subscribe.

subscription   (1) An agreement to contribute a sum of money, e.g. subscribed capital, subscription to a joint venture, a charitable donation.   (2) A payment made which is the membership fee of a club or society.

subsidiary book   (1) A book containing further details of accounts maintained in the ledger, e.g. a plant register. (2) Same as **book of original entry**.

sum of the digits method   See **depreciation methods:** *sum of the digits.*

sundry creditors   Miscellaneous liabilities at the year end requiring immediate or imminent payment but which are not included in the headings of trade creditors, long term loans (due for repayment), taxation due or dividends payable. This heading is shown under *current liabilities* in the balance sheet.

sundry debtors   Miscellaneous amounts owed to a business at the year end but which are not included in the headings of trade debtors, bank balances, loans given, or investments made. This heading is shown on the balance sheet under *current assets*. See also **accrued income** and **payments in advance**.

superannuation contributions   Amounts paid by employees out of wages or salaries to provide themselves with a pension when they retire. The majority of employers pay towards pensions for their employees but require some contribution from the employees.

surplus   (1) Assets or stocks of material or goods which are in excess of the operating requirements of a business. (2) Where income exceeds expenditure in a non-profit-making organisation, the difference is a *surplus*.

suspense account   A waiting or holding account which records any difference that arises in the books of a business due to unknown errors. The errors are those that cause the trial balance not to balance. Should the error(s) be found at a later date, corrections are made through the *journal proper*. Also used to complete the double entry temporarily when the nature of a transaction is not known at the time.

system software   A set of programs which control the internal operations of a computer and many aspects of its performance. These programs are usually built into the computer by the manufacturer.

Tt

T account   T-shaped layout of an account which has two sides — a *debit* side and a *credit* side. See illustration below.

T/A and t/a   Abbreviation for **trading as**.

tabular books   Same as **analysed books**.

tangible asset   An asset which physically exists, e.g. property, machinery and vehicles.

tax   Money that people have to pay to the state because they are required to do so by law. There are many different taxes, for example:
(a) tax based on income, called *income tax*.
(b) companies pay tax on their profits called *corporatin tax*.
(c) persons buying shares or property pay tax called *stamp duty*.
See also **money**.

tax code   A number that shows the tax allowance a person is able to set against total income in order to

T Account

T ACCOUNT

MOTOR EXPENSES ACCOUNT

M2

Debit side   Credit side

See illustration on page 47 which shows a complete account using this layout.

105

calculate the amount of income. The code number is determined by the Inland Revenue and is based on the information given to them by a tax-payer on his annual tax return form and the current personal allowances.

tax tables   Books provided by the Inland Revenue which are used by an employer to calculate the tax paid each week (or month) by employees.

taxable pay   The amount of pay calculated by the employer from the employee's code number and tax tables, upon which tax is charged.

terms of trade   The conditions upon which a seller agrees to sell goods. These conditions protect the seller in the case of future disagreements with the buyer and also show the extent of the seller's liability in the event of claims being made upon him.

three column accounts   Accounts laid out vertically rather than horizontally as in the T form of account. The three columns are for *debits*, *credits* and *balances*. See illustration below.

Three Column Account — Purchase Ledger Example

B. MADDISON PURCHASE LEDGER RECORD CARD	SUPPLIER: A. CREDDOR LIMITED UNIT 16, MORTON IND. ESTATE WITHAM, ESSEX		A/C No. C 1 Sheet No. 3
Date	Details	Debit	Credit	Balance
1 May	b/f			92.63
1 May	Invoice Nº AC567		66.70	159.33
1 May	Cheque	92.63		66.70
18 May	Invoice Nº AC588		84.06	150.76
23 May	Cheque	66.70		84.06
25 May	Invoice Nº AC601		55.20	139.26
27 May	Invoice Nº AC620		120.32	259.58
3 June	Invoice Nº AC645		75.90	335.48
	c/f			

three-in-one entry   Same as **simultaneous entry**.

time card   Same as **clock card**.

time rates   Hourly rates of pay used as the basis of calculating gross wages.

time sheet   A sheet used to record the arrival and departure times of an employee. Usually completed by the employee's supervisor or foreman. The time sheet is used by the wages staff to calculate gross wages.

total account   Same as **control account**.

total cost   A term that can have several meanings, e.g.

(a)   the total business costs which have been analysed into direct costs, production overheads and all the other overheads of sales and distribution, administration and finance;

(b)   all the costs associated with a specific project, job, order, process or department. See illustration below.

Total Cost

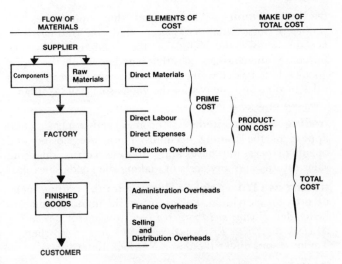

Make up of total cost in a manufacturing business.

trade creditors   Amounts owed to the suppliers of goods or services used by a business.

trade debtors   Amounts owing to a business by customers.

trade discount   See **discount types**.

trade investment   Stocks and shares acquired and held by a business in companies which are in the same industry. This term is not used often, since investment by a company must be classified in the balance sheet under separate headings of fixed assets, subsidiaries, quoted and unquoted investments.

trademarks   Trademarks are the distinguishing names or symbols used by a company which have been officially registered with the Patent Office. The cost of developing and registering trade marks is considered as a fixed asset if it has not been written off to the profit and loss account. See also **patent rights**.

trading   Buying and selling goods.

trading account   The account that summarises the profits or losses that have been made on trading. This account shows the value of the opening stocks, net purchases and closing stocks that together enable the cost of goods sold to be determined. The difference between the net sales income and the cost of the goods sold will be either a *gross loss* or a *gross profit*.

trading account items   Incomes and expenses that appear in the trading account. These are closing and opening stocks, purchases and purchase returns, sales and sales returns and any costs of making the goods saleable.

trading as (T/A or **t/a)**   This denotes the trading name used by an individual. For example, the final account will be headed *Trading and Profit and Loss Account of A Taylor T/A Newlook Enterprises for the year ended 30th June 19-9* (where A Taylor trades under the name Newlook Enterprises).

transaction   A business deal that usually involves an

agreement to provide goods or services for the payment of money.

transit   Goods or documents in the process of being moved between businesses or between branches of a business are described as *in transit*.

transposition (of figures)   Two figures recorded in the wrong order. The figure could be a two-figure number itself (e.g. 23 recorded as 32), or the two figures may be within a larger number (e.g. 1934 recorded as 1394).

trend figures   Figures that show the direction in which values are moving. For example, if the cost of a loaf of bread is successively 48p, 49p, 52p, 56p over four years then the trend is upwards.

trial balance   A list of the balances in the ledger accounts at a specific date. If the books have been entered correctly, then the total of the debit balance should equal the total of the credit balance. A trial balance is prepared to prove the accuracy of the accounts and as a basis for the preparation of the final accounts.

true and fair   Auditors are required to show on their report whether or not the accounts they have audited are true and fair. *True* means that the figures are factual. *Fair* means that the figures represent the financial position of the company and that no misrepresentation has occurred. Misrepresentation can occur where wrong accounting bases are used, information is not disclosed or wrong interpretations are made of figures.

true purchases figure   Same as **net purchases**.

true sales figure   Same as **net sales**.

turnover   Same as **sales**.

two column cash book   A simple cash book that records *cash* receipts and payments and *bank* receipts and payments. The name *two column* refers to the two columns on both the debit side of each page (to record receipts) and the credit side (to record payments), i.e. the two different ledger accounts of cash and bank are recorded on one sheet.

Uu

uncalled capital   The total amount that shareholders have not yet been asked to pay on shares issued to them. See also **called-up capital**.

undersubscription   The situation that exists when a company wishing to issue share capital seeks applications for shares and fewer shares are applied for than are available. Opposite of **oversubscription**.

undistributed profits   All the profits made are owed to shareholders, but directors do not have to pay all of the profits to them. Profits that have not been paid to shareholders but have been retained in the company are called undistributed profits. Profit may be retained for various purposes, e.g. (a) to buy new assets; (b) to replace worn out assets; (c) to meet possible future losses; (d) to pay dividends to shareholders when (in future years) profits are low; (e) to expand the business.

unpresented cheques   Cheques written out by an account holder and sent to suppliers or paid for services received, but not yet passed to the account holder's bank for payment.

unquoted investment   Investments made by an investor (an individual or a company) in a business which does not have its shares quoted on the Stock Exchange.

Vv

valuation of investment   The realisable value of investments held. In the case of an investment in a public company, the share price can be determined from the Stock Exchange, but for private limited companies and non-incorporated businesses such a valuation is difficult.

valuation of stock   Same as **stock valuation**.

Value Added Tax   A tax on the supply of goods and services made by a registered taxable person. A registered taxable person means any sole trader or company involved in the supply of goods and services which are not exempt supplies. However, although most goods and services are standard rated (15%), some may be zero-rated. See also **exempt rating, standard rate** and **zero rating**.

variable cost   A cost which varies in direct proportion to the output or activity of a business. For example, the quantity of direct material used in manufacturing a product will vary directly according to the number of products actually manufactured.

variable expenses   Same as **variable cost**.

variance analysis   This is an analysis of the differences that arise between actual costs incurred and the standard costs or budgeted costs with which they are compared. The differences (variances) are investigated to find out why they have occurred. If the standard cost was fixed correctly then either some inefficiency or unforeseen difficulty has arisen (if the actual costs are higher) or some extra efficiency or unforeseen benefit has arisen (if the costs are lower).

VAT   Abbreviation for **Value Added Tax**.

VDU   Abbreviation for **visual display unit**.

vertical presentation   A method of laying out the details underneath each other when displaying accounts and balance sheets. This layout is used mainly when presenting the final accounts and balance sheet for the owner or shareholders. Three column accounts are also examples of vertical presentation. See illustration of **balance sheet** on page 10.

vertical accounts   Same as **vertical presentation**.

visual display unit (VDU)   A piece of computer hardware that looks similar to a television screen and displays information for the computer user. Examples of information displayed are:
(a)   data being entered;
(b)   stored data;
(c)   the results of problem-solving exercises;
(d)   menus.
Also known as **visual display terminal** or **visual display device**.

voluntary deductions   Amounts taken from the gross pay of employees at their request, by the employer, e.g. savings, repayments of loans, trade union subscriptions.

voluntary winding up   See **creditors' voluntary winding up** and **members' voluntary winding up**.

voucher   A document that is proof of an expense having been incurred. A receipt obtained upon purchase (e.g. a petrol bill) is a voucher. Some expenses will be incurred for which no receipts are issued (e.g. taxi fares and train fares). In such cases, the employee who is reimbursed with the money spent will have to sign a voucher showing the expense incurred. The voucher then acts as proof that the cashier has paid out that sum of money. An invoice is also a voucher. See illustration of **petty cash voucher**.

Ww

wages   The money earned by employees who work for an employer. A *basic wage* usually refers to the earnings for working the required number of hours in the week. To this may be added overtime and bonuses, additional sums for working shift or nights. The total earnings for the week are called *gross wages*. After deductions have been made (both statutory and voluntary) the amount received by an employee is called **net pay**.

wages accrued   Wages owing at the end of a financial period. When a business closes its books at the end of the year, some expenses are likely to be owing. If the year ends (for example) on a Thursday and wages are paid on a Friday, the wages earned for the days of the week up to and including Thursday, are shown on the balance sheet as *wages accrued*.

wages book   The weekly record of employee's gross wages and deductions.

wages package   A set of programs which enable storage and update of information about employees (such as name, tax code, deductions) and from which the weekly or monthly payroll for employees can be calculated. Other features may include: (a) printing the payslips; (b) printing a list of required cheque payments; (c) printing a note and coin analysis.

wages systems   Rules and procedures which determine how the gross wage of employees are to be calculated, e.g. a time rate system, a piecework system.

warehouse expenses   The costs of operating a warehouse. A company selling goods nationally will operate a number of warehouse and distribution centres where the products it sells are kept until sold. The costs of operating such centres are often large and the company, in its bookkeeping procedures, would keep these expenses separate in order to measure and control them.

WDA   Abbreviation for **writing down allowance**.

WDV   Abbreviation for **written down value**.

winding up   The name of the procedure that operates when a business or company closes down. This involves assets being realised, payment to creditors paid and the return of the owner's capital. See also **compulsory winding up, members' voluntary winding up** and **creditors' voluntary winding up**.

work in progress   The stock of a manufactured business which is partly manufactured or partly completed.

Working Capital

How working capital circulates.

working capital   That part of the assets owned by a company which is available for the company to use in its daily financial activities is known as *working capital*. It is the excess of current assets over current liabilities. Same as **net current assets**. See illustration on page 114.

working capital ratio   The ratio of current assets to current liabilities. It is a measure of how much capital is readily available to meet the daily financial requirements above that needed to pay current liabilities. Same as **current ratio**.

works cost   Same as **production cost**.

works overhead   Same as **production overheads**.

write-it-once records   Same as **simultaneous accounting period**.

writing down allowance (WDA)   The allowance given by the Inland Revenue in place of depreciation when calculating the taxable profit.

written down value (WDV)   (1) The value of an asset to the business after deducting the total depreciation so far written off to the profit and loss account. This is the value shown on the balance sheet. Same as **net book value**.   (2) The value of the asset to the business for tax purposes. This value is calculated on the cost less the total writing down allowance given by the Inland Revenue.

Yy

year-end accounts   The accounts prepared at the end of the accounting period of a business, usually called the **final accounts.**

Zz

zero-rating (VAT)   The VAT rate applied to specific categories of goods, e.g. food, water and power. The rate is zero which means that the consumer pays no tax. Unlike the supplier of exempt goods and services, the supplier of zero-rated goods is entitled to reclaim VAT that he or she has paid on his or her expenses.